The People of
CENTRAL SCOTLAND
at Home and Abroad
1800-1850

By
David Dobson

CLEARFIELD

Copyright © 2022
by David Dobson
All Rights Reserved

Published for Clearfield Company by
Genealogical Publishing Company
Baltimore, Maryland
2022

ISBN: 9780806359526

INTRODUCTION

Central Scotland includes the counties of Stirlingshire and neighbouring Clackmannanshire, which stretch from Loch Lomond and the Trossachs to the upper reaches of the River Forth; the region is partly in the Highlands and partly in the Lowlands.

In the late eighteenth century, the regional economy was based on farming, textiles, and mining. The existence of iron and coal enabled industrialisation to occur relatively early. For example, the Carron Iron Works, near Falkirk, Stirlingshire, were established there in 1760 to exploit the local reserves of coal and iron. That factory is considered to mark the beginning of the Industrial Revolution in Scotland, and its most famous product was a short barrelled, rapid firing naval gun known as the carronade. The invention of the hot-blast process by James Beaumont Neilson in 1828 cut costs, increased productivity, and used raw coal, which enabled the iron industry to flourish. At the same time coalmining was rapidly expanding due to domestic demand and industrial expansion, especially the adoption of the Bolton and Watt steam engines in Scottish textile mills. While the local textile industry was initially domestic with hand loom weavers working at home, industrialization soon brought about the establishment of textile factories. Supplies of flax were imported from the Baltic and the linen manufactured became an important export for Central Scotland. The nearly simultaneous Agricultural Revolution caused the merging of small farms, creating a rural labour surplus that either moved to the burgeoning factory towns in the Lowlands or emigrated.

Most of the early emigration from Central Scotland was by individuals or family groups, but in 1773 the Arnprior Emigration Society formed by farmers in west Stirlingshire organised an emigration to Vermont. In the early nineteenth century three other emigration societies in Stirlingshire--Alloa in 1817, Balfron in 1821, and Deanston in 1821--organised groups of emigrants bound for Upper Canada.

This book identifies people from the counties of Stirlingshire and Clackmannanshire, at home and abroad, between 1800 and 1850. The entries, to some extent, enable family historians in the Americas, Australasia, and other locations, to link with their kin who remained in

Scotland. The Statistical Account of Scotland [the OSA], compiled between 1791 and 1799, and the New Statistical Account [the NSA], compiled between 1832 and 1845, are especially helpful for understanding Scottish society of the period. These can be consulted in major libraries, such as the National Library of Scotland, or online.

The List of Abbreviations begins on page 128.

David Dobson

Dundee, Scotland, 2022

Stirling Castle

The town of Stirling

The town of Stirling

The town of Alloua

Wallace Monument

ABERCROMBY, HENRY, a maltman, was admitted as a burgess and guilds-brother of Stirling on 14 October 1793. [SBR]

ABRAMS, WILLIAM, master of the Dunlop of Grangemouth trading between Greenock and Quebec in 1812/1814/1815/. [NRS.E504.15.93/96/101/104/07]

ADAM, ALEXANDER, master of the Mariner of Grangemouth trading between Port Glasgow and Miramachi, New Brunswick, in 1818, and between Greenock and Chaleur Bay, New Brunswick, in 1828. [NRS.E504.28.101/163]

ADAM, Lady CHARLES, of Blair Adam Estate, Stirlingshire, 1831. [SJA.10/2.4C]

ADAM, Sir CHARLES, MP for Clackmannanshire and Kinross, 1831. [SJA.8/12.1C]

ADAM, GEORGE, a maltman, was admitted as a burgess and guilds-brother of Stirling on 27 August 1796. [SBR]

ADAM, HENRY, son of Robert Adam in Springbank, Falkirk, Stirlingshire, died in Grenada on 29 October 1861. [SGS]

ADAM, ROBERT, Provost of Falkirk, Stirlingshire, 1849. [SJA.9/11.4E]

ADAM. ROBERT, agent of the National Bank of Scotland in Falkirk, Stirlingshire, in 1849. [POD]

ADAM, WILLIAM, of Blair Adam, Stirlingshire, in 1836. [SJA.12/8,4D]

AIKMAN, ..., a bailie of Stirling in 1841. [SJA.9/4.4D]

AITCHISON, LAWRENCE, a clock and watchmaker in Falkirk from 1836 to 1852. [OSC.108]

AITKEN, ANN, born 1801, wife of James McLay, died in New Zealand on 4 December 1869. [Killearn gravestone, Stirlingshire]

AITKEN, LAUCHLAN, MD, born 18 March 1844 in Gartcows, Falkirk, Stirlingshire, died in Rome, Italy, on 27 December 1853. [Rome Protestant gravestone]

AITKEN, THOMAS, in Falkirk, Stirlingshire, in 1834. [SJA.21/11.4C]

AITKEN, WILLIAM, a smith in Cambusbarron, Stirlingshire, in 1853. [SJA.20/5.2E]

AITKEN, ROBERT, a clerk at Stirling station, in 1852. [SJA.22/10, 4C]

ALEXANDER, EDWARD, a maltman, was admitted as a burgess and guilds-brother of Stirling on 19 June 1793. [SBR]

ALEXANDER, EDWARD MAYNE, born 16 December 1840 in Halifax, Nova Scotia, died in St Leonard's on 1 August 1916. [Logie Old gravestone, Stirlingshire]

ALEXANDER, JAMES, a merchant in St John's, Canada, son and heir of Margaret Morison or Alexander in Alloa, Clackmannanshire, in 1830. [NRS.S/H]

ALEXANDER, JOHN, of Little Kerse, Stirling, in 1841. [SJA.14/5,1F]

ALEXANDER, JOHN, in Sydney, Australia, married Elisabeth Cassels, in Arnprior, Australia, 25 March 1847. [SO]

ALEXANDER, MARGARET, c/o Mrs Ross in Friars Wynd, Stirling, was accused of theft in 1837. [NRS.AD14.37.207]

ALEXANDER, WILLIAM PATERSON, a watch and clockmaker in Balfron, Stirlingshire, 1836 to 1870. [OSC.108]

ALISON, A. ALEXANDER, in Stirling, in 1846. [SJA.17/7.4C]

ALLAN, HELEN, born 1786 in Alloa, Clackmannanshire, died 10 April 1849, in Leith, wife of Captain James Lindsay. [South Leith gravestone]

ALLAN, JAMES, and Elizabeth Colvin, 1791. [Falkirk gravestone, Stirlingshire]

ALLAN, JOHN, in Stirling in 1824. [SJA.10/6,4C]

ALLAN, Reverend R. in Tillicoultry, Clackmannanshire, in 1826. [SJA.24/8.4B]

ALLAN, WILLIAM, born 1763 in Stirlingshire, educated at Glasgow University, emigrated to Charleston, South Carolina, in 1780, a merchant in S.C., died 1827. [Old Scots gravestone, Charleston]

ALSTON, THOMAS, was admitted as a burgess and guilds-brother of Stirling on 14 July 1792. [SBR]

ANDERSON, ALEXANDER, in Thornville, North America, heir to his grandfather John Kerr, a mason in Camelon, Stirlingshire, who died in 1817. [NRS.S/H]

ANDERSON, ANDREW, master of the Phoebe of Kincardine, trading between Alloa, Clackmannanshire, and Copenhagen, Denmark, in 1815. [NRS.E504.2.13]

ANDERSON, GEORGE, born 1820 in Kincardine-on-Forth, a merchant who settled in Guelph, Ontario, in 1856, died in Harrison, Ontario, on 26 December 1890. [FFP]

ANDERSON, JAMES, was admitted as a burgess and guilds-brother of Stirling on 25 December 1790. [SBR]

ANDERSON, JAMES, was admitted as a burgess and guilds-brother of Stirling on 5 February 1799. [SBR]

ANDERSON, JAMES, born 1785 in Falkirk, Stirlingshire, applied to settle in Canada in 1817. [TNA.CO384.3]

ANDERSON, JAMES, in Alleghany, USA, grandson and heir of James Anderson, a farmer in Boghouse, Kilsyth, Stirlingshire, who died in 1833. [NRS.S/H]

ANDERSON, Sir JAMES, in Stirling in 1853. [SJA.11/2.3B]

ANDERSON, JANET, shopkeeper to the late Mrs Littlejohn in Stirling, testament, 1794, Comm. Stirling. [NRS]

ANDERSON, JOHN, was admitted as a burgess and guilds-brother of Stirling on 16 January 1796. [SBR]

ANDERSON, JOHN, born 1793 in Camelon, Falkirk, Stirlingshire, son of John Anderson and his wife Janet Stean, fought in the Uprising of

1820 at Bonnymuir, found guilty of rebellion and was transported to New South Wales, Australia for life in 1821, a schoolmaster to the Scots Presbyterian community at Portland Head from 1823 until his death on 16 July 1858. [Ebenezer gravestone, Hawkesbury River, NSW] [TSR]

ANDERSON, LAURENCE, born 1845, youngest son of William Anderson a wood merchant in Kincardine on Forth, died in Sundswall, Sweden, on 3 October 1884. [S.12870]

ANDERSON, MARGARET, wife of James Thomson, died at Springbank, Denny, Stirlingshire, 16 June 1853. [SO]

ANDERSON, ROBERT, died in San Francisco, California, on 21 April 1853. [SO]

ANDERSON, THOMAS, born 1818, died in Melbourne, Victoria, Australia, on 16 May 1888. [Larbert gravestone, Stirlingshire]

ANDERSON, WILLIAM, Provost of Stirling, in 1830. [SJA.28/1,4A]

ANDERSON, WILLIAM, master of the St Andrew of Stirling trading between Montrose, Angus, and Alloa, Clackmannanshire, in 1814. [NRS.E504.2.13]

ANDERSON, WILLIAM, master of the Alexander of Kincardine, trading between Alloa, Clackmannanshire, and Pillau, Prussia, in 1817. [NRS.E504.2.13]

ANDERSON, Reverend, in St Ninian's, Stirling, in 1833. [SJA.10/1.4C]

ANDREW, Reverend James of the Dunblane Congregational Chapel in 1831. [SJA.6/1,3C]

ANGUS, WILLIAM, born 1780 in Stirling, a carpenter who settled in Brooklyn, New York, was naturalised on 7 November 1826. [NY Marine Court]

ANSTRUTHER, JAMES, in Tillicoultry, Clackmannanshire, in 1842. [SJA.23/12, 4D]

ARBUCKLE, WILLIAM, in Falkirk, Stirlingshire, nephew and heir of John Steven a millwright in Trinidad, 1845. [NRS.S/H]

ARCHIBALD, JAMES, born 1843, a master painter, died in Boston, USA, on 16 December 1916. [Alloa gravestone, Clackmannanshire]

ARCHIBALD, MARGARET, daughter of Alexander Armstrong, [1798-1878], and his wife Mary ......, [1799-1873], died in St Louis, Illinois, on 2 February 1835. [Tullibody gravestone, Clackmannanshire]

ARCHIBALD, WILLIAM, born 1842, a watch-maker and jeweller, 18 Port Street, Stirling, died 1893. [OSC.61]

ARMSTRONG, JAMES, from Stirling, died in Halifax, Nova Scotia, on 12 April 1842. [Acadian Recorder. 16.4.1842].12811]

ARMSTRONG, ROBERT, Precentor of Kippen Parish Church, Stirlingshire, in 1849. [SJA.6/7,4D]

ARNOT, DAVID HENRY, born 1822, son of Henry Arnot, [1786-1842], a surgeon in the Service of the East India Company, and his wife Margaret Oliphant, [1789-1853], an architect who died in New York on 2 November 1853. [Dollar gravestone, Clackmannanshire]

AULD, WILLIAM, died at Kippen, Stirlingshire, on 28 January 1841. [SO]

BACHOP, JOHN, was admitted as a burgess and guilds-brother of Stirling on 1 December 1792. [SBR]

BAIN, FRANCIS, died in Grenada on 8 December 1836. [SO]

BAIRD, GEORGE, in Falkirk, a candidate for the Falkirk District of Burghs in 1851. [SJA.24/1,1E]

BAIRD, JAMES, was admitted as a burgess and guilds-brother of Stirling on 23 September 1797. [SBR]

BAIRD, JAMES, master of the Helen of Kincardine trading between Alloa, Clackmannanshire, and Pillau, Prusssia, in 1816. [NRS.E504.2.13]

BAIRD, JANET, born 1835, daughter of Alexander Baird and his wife Ann Paton, died in South Australia, on 30 October 1878. [Holy Rude gravestone, Stirling]

BAIRD, JOHN, born 1796, son of James Baird, [1772-1831], and his wife Helen Gray, [1783-1821], died on Nevis on 5 February 1814. [Tulliallan gravestone]

BAIRD, JOHN, born 1832, son of Alexander Baird and his wife Ann Paton, died in New Zealand, on 30 October 1869. [Holy Rude gravestone, Stirling]

BAIRD, MARY, died at Bridge of Allan, Stirlingshire, on 13 February 1840. [SO]

BAIRD, Major PATRICK, in Stirling in 1842. [SJA.28/10,4E]

BAIRD, ROBERT, a skipper in Dunmore, Falkland, Stirlingshire, testament, 1801, Comm. Stirling. [NRS]

BAIRD, WILLIAM, born 1750 in Stirling, a carpenter, died in St John, New Brunswick, on 5 April 1833. [Weekly Observer, 9.4.1833]

BALFOUR, HELEN GORDON, born 1849, second daughter of John Balfour of Devon Bank, Alloa, Clackmannanshire, died in Thornton, Illinois, on 18 July 1854. [W.XV.1571]

BALFOUR, ROBERT, a soldier, died at Southfield, Stirling, 11 February 1847. [SO]

BALFOUR, THOMAS, was admitted as a burgess and guilds-brother of Stirling on 17 May 1794. [SBR]

BALFOUR, WALTER, born in St Ninian's, Stirling, in 1776, emigrated as a minister to America in 1806, a member of the Scots Charitable Society of Boston in 1817, died in Charlestown, Massachusetts, in 1852. [SCS/NEHGS]

BALLOCH, JAMES, born 1764 in St Ninian's, Stirlingshire, emigrated to America in 1790, died 27 February 1831. [CFG]

BANEMAN, ANDREW, a distiller in Tulliallan in 1834. [SJA.5/12,3D]

BANKS, CHRISTIAN, born 1732, died in Stirling on 22 September 1819. [SM.85]

BANKS, Reverend JOHN, born 1763 in Stirling, son of John Banks a merchant in Kilwinning, educated at Glasgow University in 1787, a minister in Edinburgh, emigrated to America in 1796, a minister in New York state from 1796 to 1816, settled in Montgomery County, 1820 until his death on 10 April 1826 in Philadelphia, Pennsylvania. [AP][MAGU][UPC]

BARNTON, W. R., in Stirling in 1837. [SJA.3/10.3G]F

BARCLAY, WILLIAM, son of James Barclay, [1800-1854], and his wife Mary Smollett, [1813-1904], settled in Halifax, Nova Scotia. [Alva gravestone, Clackmannanshire]

BARLAND, PETER, a surgeon, died at Craigmill, Stirling, on 12 June 1845. [SO]

BARR, JANET, died at the Mill of Campsie, Stirlingshire, on 22 November 1838. [SO]

BARR, ..., of Aithrey Wells, Stirlingshire, in 1846. [SJA.10/7,1A]

BARTHOLOMEW, JAMES, born 1805, died on 22 June 1849, husband of Ann Brown, born in 1801, died on 3 July 1890. [Muiravonside gravestone, Stirlingshire]

BATHGATE, SIMON, Ensign of the Loyal Stirling Volunteers, was admitted as a burgess and guilds-brother of Dunfermline, Fife, on 17 July 1804. [DM]

BAUCHOP, WILLIAM, born 1749, a farmer in Boquhan, died 24 April 1837, husband of Margaret McLachlan, born 1769, died 17 November 1836. [Balfron gravestone, Stirlingshire]

BAXTER, JAMES, in Stirling in 1827. [SJA.15/3,4E]

BAXTER, WILLIAM, a hammerman, was admitted as a burgess and guilds-brother of Stirling on 20 July 1793. [SBR]

BAYNE, JOHN, a watchmaker and clockmaker in Spittal Street, Stirling, from 1777 until 1790, husband of Margaret Campbell, born 1757, died 11 October 1840. [OSC.62]

BAYNE, JOHN, an Excise officer, died in Clackmannan on 18 January 1838. [SO]

BAYNE, THOMAS, son of William Bayne and his wife Agnes Blair in Doune, Stirlingshire, settled in Idaho before 1859. [NRS.S/H]

BAYNE, WILLIAM, died in Barbados on 6 August 1840. [SO]

BELCH, JOHN, was admitted as a burgess and guilds-brother of Stirling on 24 January 1798. [SBR]

BELCH, PETER, son of Peter Belch a merchant in Stirling, was educated at Glasgow University in 1785, an advocate in 1793, admitted as a burgess and guilds-brother of Stirling on 19 February 1799, died in Kingston, Jamaica, on 8 March 1808. [MAGU] [SBR]

BELL, DAVID, born 1778, a watch and clockmaker in Stirling from 1801 to 1850. [OSC.62]

BELL, Captain, master of the Thames of Alloa from Alloa, Clackmannanshire, to Quebec in 1849 and 1850. [EEC]JA.19/11, 4B]

BENNET, ALEXANDER, in Alloa, Clackmannanshire, in 1858. [SJA.26/2,5B]

BENNET, GEORGE, eldest son of Reverend Patrick Bennet in Polmont, Stirlingshire, settled in Charleston, South Carolina, around 1783. [NRS.RD4.236.795]

BENNET, WILLIAM, the Sheriff Substitute for Clackmannanshire in 1852. [SJA]

BENNY, JOHN, was admitted as a burgess and guilds-brother of Stirling on 16 October 1798. [SBR]

BENNIE, THOMAS, a schoolteacher in Coalsnaughton, Tillicoultry, Clackmannanshire, was accused of obstructing, assaulting, officers of the law in 1818. [NRS.AD.14.18.49]

BEVERIDGE, THOMAS, from Alloa, Clackmannanshire, a theological student in 1776, emigrated to America in 1783, a minister in Cambridge, New York, died there in 1798. [Records of the United Presbyterian Church]

BEVERAGE, Captain, master of the Pomona of Alloa from Alloa, Clackmannanshire, to Quebec in 1840. [EEC]

BIGGAM, HAMILTON, born 1799 in Doune, Stirlingshire, a merchant who was naturalised in New York on 10 October 1826. [NY Marine Court]

BISHOP, W., in Falkirk, Stirlingshire, applied to settle in Canada on 27 February 1815. [NRS.RH9]

BLACK, ANDREW, master of the Delight of Alloa trading between Alloa, Clackmannanshire, and Riga, Latvia, in 1816; master of the Freedom of Alloa trading between Alloa and St Petersburg, Russia, in 1817. [NRS.E504.2.13]

BLACK, JAMES, born 1789 in Stirlingshire, died in Cornwallis, Nova Scotia, on 9 March 1839. [Acadian Recorder, 16.3.1839]

BLACK, WILLIAM, of Coilchat, Doune, Stirlingshire, in 1839. [SJA.13/9,4E]

BLACKBURN, JOHN, son of John Blackburn of Killearn, [1756-1840], settled in Jamaica. [Killearn gravestone, Stirlingshire]

BLACKBURN, PETER, MP of Stirlingshire in 1855. [SJA.23/2, 7C]

BLACKBURN, ..., of Killearn, Stirlingshire, in 1852. [SJA.29/10.4C]

BLACKWOOD, HELEN, wife of John Weir in Grahamston, Falkirk, Stirlingshire, dead by 1853, mother of John Blackwood Weir in Torwodhall, Canada. [NRS.S/H]

BLACKWOOD, JAMES, in Dollar, Clackmannanshire, versus Reverend Andrew Milne, summons, 1842. [NRS.CS97.B.3.4]

BLAIR, AGNES, wife of William Bayne a grocer in Doune, Stirlingshire, mother of Thomas Bayne in Idaho, dead by 1859. [NRS.S/H]

BLAIR, ANDREW, born 1787 in Stirlingshire, husband of Janet born 1793 in Glasgow, parents of Thomas R. Blair born 1815 in Glasgow, emigrated via Liverpool to America, were naturalised in New York on 11 May 1821. [NY Court of Common Pleas]

BLAIR, BUCHANAN, born 1793, a labourer from Doune, Stirlingshire, emigrated via Port Glasgow aboard the Favourite of St John bound for St John, New Brunswick, on 22 October 1815. [PANB.ms23E.9798]9

BLAIR, JOHN, President of the Balfron Emigration Society, Stirlingshire, with his wife, two sons, and four daughters, from Greenock aboard the David of London bound for Quebec, Canada, on 19 May 1821, was granted land in Lanark, Upper Canada on 3 September 1821. [PAO]

BLAIR, JOHN G., a merchant, eldest son of William Blair, died in Sengerties, New York, on 31 October 1839. [SG.8/823]

BLAIR, JOHN, a gardener in Doune, Stirlingshire, in 1849. [SJA.25/5,4D]

BOOSIE, DAVID, of Parkhead near Alloa, Clackmannanshire, in 1846. [SJ.27/11.4D]

BORLAND, ROBERT, died on 8 April 1848, husband of Margaret Leishman, parents of William Borland, who was drowned at Sierra Leone on 11 February 1851. [Larbert gravestone, Stirlingshire]

BORTHWICK, JOHN, in Grangemouth in 1846. [SJA.30/10,4E]

BOWIE, JOHN, a clock and watchmaker in Falkirk in 1800. [OSC.108]

BOWIE, JOHN, a wright in Stirling around 1811. [OSC.63]

BOWIE, ROBERT, a smith who settled in Tortula in the Virgin Islands by 1792, [Kincardine, Blair Drummond gravestone, Stirlingshire]

BOWIE, ROBERT, born 1813, eldest son of Alexander Bowie a builder in Stirling, died in Kingston, Jamaica, on 17 April 1833. [SG.149]

BOWIE, ROBERT, a wright in Stirling around 1817. [OSC.63]

BOYD, JOHN, master of the brigantine Lady Keith of Kincardine testament, 1824, Comm. Dunblane. [NRS]

BOYD, WILLIAM, died in Westmoreland, Jamaica, on 5 September 1850. [SO]

BRAND, GEORGE, born 1821, a potato dealer in Larbert, Stirlingshire, was accused of theft and reset in 1852. [NRS.AD14.14.52.373]

BRECHAN, JAMES, was admitted as a burgess and guilds-brother of Stirling on 27 April 1790. [SBR]

BREMBER, PETER, was admitted as a burgess and guilds-brother of Stirling on 8 October 1790. [SBR]

BREMBER, WILLIAM, a weaver in Alva, Stirlingshire, was accused of poaching in 1844. [NRS.AD14.44.390]

BREMNER, GEORGE, sr., President of the Deanston Emigration Society, Stirlingshire, with four sons and two daughters, from Greenock aboard the David of London bound for Quebec, Canada, on 19 May 1821, was granted land in Lanark, Upper Canada by 6 August 1821. [PAO]

BREMNER, GEORGE, jr., of the Deanston Emigration Society, Stirlingshire, with his wife, a son and a daughter, from Greenock aboard the David of London bound for Quebec, Canada, on 19 May 1821, was granted land in Lanark, Upper Canada by 6 August 1821. [PAO]

BRODIE, ALEXANDER, born 1788, died in Stirling on 10 July 1869, husband of Louisa Mercer, born in 1799, died at Eskbank near Edinburgh, on 8 February 1881. [Logie Old gravestone, Stirlingshire]

BRODIE, FRANCIS WALKER, born 1826, Captain and commander of the Malwa contingent Cavalry, was killed by mutineers at Mullarghur on 7 June 1857. [Logie Old gravestone, Stirlingshire]

BRODIE, GEORGE FRANCIS, born in 1834, died on a voyage from China on 19 January 1848. [Logie Old gravestone, Stirlingshire]

BRODIE, GRAEME, MERCER, born in 1823, a Lieutenant of the 52nd Bengal Native Infantry, died at Gawhattee, Upper Assam, India, on 3 January 1848. [Logie Old gravestone, Stirlingshire]

BRODIE, JOHN PRINGLE, born 1806 in Alloa, son of William Brodie, [1780-1846], a schoolmaster, and his wife Isabella Plowman, [1784-1858], settled in Mexico by 1851, died in San Francisco, California, on 30 October 1868. [Alloa gravestone, Clackmannanshire]

BRODIE, WILLIAM MERCER, born 1819, Captain of the 7th Bombay Native Infantry, died at Sholapore on 3 May 1860. [Logie Old gravestone, Stirlingshire]

BROOKMAN, WILLIAM, at Lock 16, Camelon, Stirlingshire, in 1848. [SJA.14/4,4E]

BROOKS, JOHN, son of John Brooks, [1811-1848], and his wife Marjory Taylor, [1814-1847], settled in Australia. [Kincardine Blair Drummond gravestone, Stirlingshire]

BROOM, DAVID, landlord of the Red Lion Inn in Falkirk, Stirlingshire, in 1831. [SJA.29/12,1E]

BROTHERSON, Mrs BARBARA, in Touch, Stirlingshire, widow Of Ludovic Brotherson in St Kitts, heir of her brother Archibald Brotherson of Touch, who died in 1818. [NRS.S/H]

BROUGH, WILLIAM, a clock and watchmaker in Kilsyth around 1800. [OSC.109]

BROWN, ALEXANDER, gardener to Captain Fairfoul at Roman Camp near Callendar, Stirlingshire, versus Helen Wilson, daughter of John Wilson, a wheelwright in Alloa, residing with Robert Binnie, a merchant in Stirling, a Process of Divorce in 1804. [NRS.CC8.6.1181]

BROWN, DANIEL, a skinner in Stirling, testament, 1792, Comm. Stirling. [NRS]

BROWN, DAVID, a merchant in St Petersburg, Russia, son of John Brown in Greenhowe, Stirlingshire, married Hannah Cassels, [1762-1859], in Leith in 1791, [SM.53.307]; he was admitted as a burgess and guilds-brother of Edinburgh in 1792, [EBR]

BROWN, Captain DAVID, of Park, residing in Stirling, eldest son of David Brown a writer in Melrose, Roxburghshire, nephew and heir of John Brown of Park, Roxburghshire, 1827. [NRS.S/H]

BROWN, EBENEZER, in Stirling, graduated MD from King's College, Aberdeen, on 22 January 1825. [KCA]

BROWN, EBENEZER, of Braendam, Thornhill, in 1828. [SJA.27/11, 4B]

BROWN, GEORGE, of Carron, Stirlingshire, in 1859. [SJA.10/6, 4E]

BROWN, JAMES, Captain of the Loyal Stirling Volunteers, was admitted as a burgess and guilds-brother of Dunfermline, Fife, on 17 July 1804. [DM]

BROWN, JOHN, a brewer in Stirling, testament, 1798, Comm. Stirling. [NRS]

BROWN, JOHN, master of the Dunlop of Grangemouth trading between Greenock and Halifax, Nova Scotia, and St John, New Brunswick, in 1817. [NRS.E504.15.93]

BROWN, RALPH, in Stirling in 1844. [SJA.6/12,4C]

BROWN, ROBERT, a mason in Doune, Stirlingshire, Master of the Lodge St James number 171 from 1832-1833, father of James Brown a baker. [DHN.iii]

BROWN, ROBERT, of the Alloa Glassworks, Clackmannanshire, versus John Johnstone, in 1816. [NRS.AC8.5618]

BROWN, THOMAS, in Stirling in 1850. [SJA.29/3,4C]

BROWN, Dr W. A. F., in Stirling in 1834. [SJA.4/4,4C]

BROWN, ……, brother of William Brown in Falkirk, Stirlingshire, settled in Jamaica before 1823. [NRS.CS44.1824]

BROWNING, Reverend ARCHIBALD, in Tillicoultry, Clackmannanshire, in 1833. [SJA.16/8,4B]

BROWNLEE, JAMES, eldest son of Reverend James Brownlee in Falkirk, Stirlingshire, was educated at the University of Glasgow from

1817 to 1822, graduated MA, emigrated to the USA as a probationer of the Secession Church, later a minister on Staten Island or Long Island, New York. [MAGU.296][UPC]

BRUCE, ALEXANDER, from Polmont Bank, Falkirk, Stirlingshire, died in Hopewall, St Mary's, Jamaica, on 24 July 1841. [EEC.20267]

BRUCE, DAVID, was admitted as a burgess and guilds-brother of Stirling on 3 March 1796. [SBR]

BRUCE, ELIZABETH AGNES, daughter of Alexander Bruce of Polmont, Stirlingshire, died in Hamilton, Canada West, on 12 November 1877. [EC.29087]

BRUCE, GEORGE ABERCROMBY, born 1798, second son of Alexander Bruce of Kennet, Stirlingshire, died in Tulloch, Jamaica, on 14 November 1817. [S.56.17]

BRUCE, JAMES, of Kinnaird, born in 1731, 'The celebrated traveller', died on 27 April 1794, husband of Mary Dundas. [Larbert gravestone, Stirlingshire]

BRUCE, JAMES, a Surgeon to the Forces, son of John Bruce, the Sheriff Substitute of Clackmannanshire, died on Mustique in 1796. [SM.58.577]

BRUCE, JAMES, of Bellsdyke, died in Ohio on 25 January 1849. [SO]

BRUCE, JOHN, a merchant in Grenada, son of John Bruce of Tulligarth the Sheriff Substitute of Clackmannanshire, appointed James Greig, a Writer to the Signet, as his attorney. Deed refers to Adam Wilson in Bankhead of Tullibole, and Reverend Sir Henry Moncreiff Wellwood of Tullibole, 1819. [NRS.RD5.159.216]

BRUCE, ROBERT, of Kennet, MP for Clackmannanshire and Kinross in 1834. [SJA.26/12,1C]

BRUCE, ROBERT, born 8 December 1796 at Kennet, served in the Grenadier Guards in the Peninsula War and at the Battle of Waterloo in 1815, died at Kennet on 13 August 1864, husband of .... Murray, born on 2 August 1802 at Polmaise, died at Kennet on 19 May 1846, daughter of William Murray. [Clackmannan gravestone]

BRUCE, WILLIAM, schoolmaster of the Free Church school in Doune, Stirlingshire from 1846 until his death in 1852. [DHN.98]

BRYCE, JAMES, a maltman, was admitted as a burgess and guildsbrother of Stirling on 23 September 1797. [SBR]

BRYCE, MACKIE, a shipmaster in Alloa, Clackmannanshire, testament, 1817, Comm. Stirling. [NRS.CC21]SJA.31/7,2F]

BRYCE, MACKIE, master of the Aimwell of Alloa, testament, 1827, Comm. Edinburgh. [NRS]

BRYDIE, THOMAS, agent of the Union Bank of Scotland in Alloa, Clackmannanshire, in 1849. [POD]

BRYMER, DAVID, a tourist guide in Stirling in 1857. [SJA]

BUCHAN, CHARLES, a weaver, was admitted as a burgess and guildsbrother of Stirling on 30 April 1793. [SBR]

BUCHAN, JOHN, a weaver, was admitted as a burgess and guildsbrother of Stirling on 16 June 1792. [SBR]

BUCHAN, MARY, in Stirling, dead by 1836, sister of William Buchan in Jamaica. [NRS.S/H]

BUCHANAN, ANDREW, at Stirling Bridge, testament, 1791, Comm. Stirling. [NRS]

BUCHANAN, CATHERINE, spouse to James Leckie a carter in Stirling, testament, 1798, Comm. Stirling. [NRS]

BUCHANAN, DAVID, of Bannockburn, Stirlingshire, in 1852. [SJA.24/12,4C]

BUCHANAN, DUNCAN, of Bannockburn, Stirlingshire, in 1850. [SJA1/3,4B]

BUCHANAN, JAMES, son of James Buchanan of Berryhills, was apprenticed to Henry Redpath, a clock and watch-maker in Stirling, on 1 October 1791. [OSC.64]

BUCHANAN, JANET, daughter of Dougal Buchanan of Craigievorn, Stirlingshire, married Charles McNab from Jamaica, in Edinburgh on 1 October 1792. [EMR]

BUCHANAN, JOHN, of Powis, born in 1813, late of the Bengal Civil Service, died on 18 March 1891, husband of Harriet Nimmo who died on 9 April 1892. [Logie Old gravestone, Stirlingshire]

BUCHANAN, JOHN, in Kippen, Stirlingshire, in 1837. [SJA.15/12,1B]

BUCHANAN, MARGARET, daughter of William Buchanan of Carbeth, Stirlingshire, testament, 1796, Comm. Glasgow. [NRS]

BUCHANAN, MARGARET ANN, daughter of James Kincaid Buchanan in Stirlingshire, married Reverend Nathaniel Vincent Fenn, MA of Trinity College, Cambridge, in Brantford, Canada West, on 22 December 1859. [DC.23469]

BUCHANAN, MARJORY, daughter of Patrick Buchanan a merchant in Kippen, Stirlingshire, spouse of John Yuill a workman in Glasgow, testament, 1800, Comm. Glasgow. [NRS]

BUCHANAN, ROBERT, in Stirling in 1827. [SJA.15/3,4C]

BUCHANAN, THOMAS, was admitted as a burgess and guilds-brother of Stirling on 22 September 1790. [SBR]

BUCHANAN, THOMAS, of Powis, Superintendent of Marine in Bombay, India, died on 12 May 1842, husband of Catherine Abercromby who died on 7 May 1841. [Logie Old gravestone, Stirlingshire]

BUCHANAN, WALTER, born 1795, a soldier of the 42nd [Black Watch] Regiment, was killed at the Battle of Waterloo on 18 June 1815. [Balfron gravestone]

BUCHANAN, WALTER, a writer in Dunblane in 1849. [SJA.6/4,4E]

BUCHANAN, WILLIAM, in Stirling in 1850. [SJA.29/3,4C]

BUCKLEY, SAMUEL, was admitted as a burgess and guilds-brother of Stirling on 21 July 1790. [SBR]

BUDGE, ROBERT, a soldier in Stirling Castle, testament, 1796, Comm. Stirling. [NRS]

BURD, JOHN, a maltman, was admitted as a burgess and guildsbrother of Stirling on 23 September 1797. [SBR]

BURGESS, JAMES, a maltman, was admitted as a burgess and guildsbrother of Stirling on 1 January 1791. [SBR]

BURGESS, JAMES, master of the Free Church school in Doune, Stirlingshire, from 1852 until 1855, thereafter Mathematical Professor at Doveton College, Calcutta, India. [DHN.99]

BURGES, JOHN, was apprenticed to Andrew Peddie, a clock maker in Stirling, by 1806. [OSC.64]

BURNETT, JONATHAN, a grocer from Bannockburn, Stirlingshire, was naturalised in New York on 18 June 1830. [NY Superior Court Records]

BURNS, JAMES ADAM, an apothecary and emigration officer in Stirling, in 1855, [SJA.22/6,3B]; died 5 December 1859, brother of Agnes Burns or Rae in Savanna, Georgia. [NRS.S/H]

BURNS, JOHN, an innkeeper in Falkirk, Stirlingshire, found guilty of reset, was sentenced to be transported to the colonies for 14 years, at Stirling on 9 September 1811. [SM.83.10.790]

BURNS, JOHN, a mason later a farmer, son of John Burns a farmer at West Brae, Doune, Stirlingshire, Master of the Lodge St James number 171 in 1840-1841, a deacon of the Free Kirk. [DHN.iii]

BURNS, THOMAS, in Clinton, Canada West, nephew and heir of Mary Oswald, wife of William Wilson in Larbert, Stirlingshire, later in Belfast, Ireland, who died in February 1857. [NRS.S/H]

BURREL, DAVID, died 1 June 1802. [Falkirk gravestone, Stirlingshire]

BURRELL, ROBERT, of Barnton Place, Stirling, died in Stirling on 10 July 1845. [SO]

BURT, ALEXANDER, born 1826, a moulder in Grahamston, Falkirk, Stirlingshire, was accused of theft and reset in 1852. [NRS.AD14.52.373]

BUTLER, WILLIAM, in New York, nephew and heir of George Chalmers, a manufacturer in Stirling, in 1837. [NRS.S/H]

CADDELL, PHILIP, in Stirling in 1854. [SJA.22/9,3C]

CADELL, WILLIAM, of Banton, born 16 August 1737, one of the partners of the original Carron Ironworks, died 17 September 1819. [Larbert gravestone, Stirlingshire]

CAIRNS, ANDREW, was admitted as a burgess of Stirling on 27 September 1794. [SBR]

CAIRNS, WILLIAM, born 1801, a private soldier of the 79th Regiment of Foot, in Stirling, was accused of housebreaking in Dunbar, in 1830. [NRS.AD14.30.304]

CALLANDER, J. H., of Craigforth, Stirlingshire, in 1848. [SJA.22/6,4D]

CALLANDER, THOMAS, born 1758 in Stirling, a political radical who emigrated to America in 1793, a journalist and author in Philadelphia, Pennsylvania, was drowned in the James River, at Richmond, Virginia, in 1813. [TSA]

CALLANDAR, THOMAS, master of the Mariner of Grangemouth trading between Port Glasgow and Miramachi, New Brunswick, in 1820. [NRS.E504.28.108]

CAMERON, ALEXANDER, of Chartershall Distillery, St Ninian's, Stirling, in 1849. [SJA.25/5,4D]

CAMERON, DANIEL, a hammerman, was admitted as a burgess of Stirling on 18 July 1794. [SBR]

CAMERON, DONALD, from Tasmania, Australia, married Mary Isabella Morrison, in Stirling, 10 June 1847. [SO]

CAMERON, DUNCAN, found guilty at Stirling and was sentenced to transportation to the colonies for 14 years. [NRS.GD1.959]

CAMERON, HUGH, born 1773, died 7 May 1857, husband of Mary Fisher, born 1780, died 17 June 1831. [Balfron gravestone, Stirlingshire]

CAMERON, JOHN, of The Burgh Mill in Stirling, in 1846. [SJA.13/2,4B]

CAMERON, ROBERT, born 3 January 1823, educated in the Ratisbon Seminary, Germany, in 1838, ordained as a Roman Catholic priest, died in Falkirk, Stirlingshire on 10 January 1848. [SIG.295] [RSC.I.256]

CAMERON, Captain, master of the Pomona of Alloa from Alloa, Clackmannanshire, to Quebec in 1856. [CM]

CAMPBELL, DAVID, Lieutenant Colonel of the 98th Regiment of Foot, died in Stirling, testament, 1792, Comm. Stirling. [NRS]

CAMPBELL, DAVID, born 1842, second son of Peter Campbell in Viewforth, Stirling, died in Mooresland, Barcoo, Queensland, Australia, on 25 September 1866. [AJ.6208]

CAMPBELL, HENRIETTA, from Stirling, died in Geneva, Switzerland, on 4 March 1841. [SO]

CAMPBELL, JAMES, a cordiner, was admitted as a burgess and guilds-brother of Stirling on 27 January 1794. [SBR]

CAMPBELL, Colonel JAMES, son of Robert Campbell in Middle Carse, Clackmannanshire, agent for the State Bank of North Carolina, died in Leakesville on 2 January 1822. [BM.12.250]

CAMPBELL, JANE, born 1821 in Drymen, Stirlingshire, daughter of Archibald Campbell, [170-1838], and his wife Jean Graham, [1789-854], died in Nashville, Tennessee, on 19 May 1849. [Drymen gravestone]

CAMPBELL, JOHN, was admitted as a burgess and guilds-brother of Stirling on 10 October 1797 [SBR]

CAMPBELL, JOHN, born 1815 in Kincardine-on-Forth, died in Jersey City, New Jersey, on 28 April 1871. [S.8674]

CAMPBELL, ROBERT, a writer in Stirling in 1849. [SJA.6/7,4C]

CAMPBELL, Mrs SUSANNAH, born 1762, widow of Colin Campbell formerly of H.M. Customs in Halifax, New Brunswick, died in Stirling on 13 April 1833. [Weekly Observer, 2.7.1833]

CAMPBELL, WALTER, Captain of the Loyal Stirlingshire Volunteers, was admitted as a burgess and guilds-brother of Dunfermline, Fife, on 17 July 1804. [DM]

CARMICHAEL, PETER, a confectioner and hotelier in Stirling, married Margaret Henderson, in Stirling, 28 June 1838. [SO]

CARMICHAEL, PETER, in Stirling in 1849. [SJA.30/3, 4C/D]

CARMICHAEL, Mr, a confectioner in Stirling in 1847. [SJA..8/1, 4D]

CARRICK, JAMES, son of William Carrick and his wife Margaret Gardiner in Stirling, married Adelaida Segand, daughter of Pablo Segand and his wife Maria Francisco Conard in New Orleans, Louisiana, on 19 March 1797 in Louisiana. [LGS]

CARRICK, ROBERT, was admitted as a burgess and guilds-brother of Stirling on 27 September 1792. [SBR]

CARRON, ALEXANDER, born 1788, a skipper 'who was lost in the Baltic with all the ship's company, on 27 October 1831, husband of Mary Dawson, born 1788, died 29 August 1868. [Alloa gravestone, Clackmannanshire]

CATHIE, NICOL, born on 1 September 1798, gardener at Airthrey Castle for 48 years, died there on 16 May 1876, husband of Mary Maxwell who died on 11 November 1861. [Logie Old gravestone, Stirlingshire]

CAY, ROBERT, married Annie Montgomery, in Melbourne, Australia, 16 October 1851. [SO]

CHALMERS, GEORGE, a manufacturer in Stirling, dead by 1837. [NRS.S/H]

CHALMER, Major, of Larbert House, Stirlingshire, in 1847. [SJA.29/1,4D]

CHALMERS, JOHN, a butcher in Alloa, Clackmannanshire, and his wife Margaret Newland sister and next of kin to John Newland in the parish of St Andrew, County Surrey, Jamaica, a marriage contract dated April 1816. [NRS.CS238.P7.68]

CHRISTIE, ALEXANDER, born 1758 in Alloa, Clackmannansahire, died in South Carolina on 15 July 1823. [Old Scots gravestone, Charleston]

CHRISTIE, ALEXANDER, from Stirling, married Christina Hunter, in New York, 14 December 1854. [SO]

CHRISTIE, Sir ARCHIBALD, in Stirling in 1838. [SJA.31/8.4D]

CHRISTIE, JAMES, a cordiner, was admitted as a burgess of Stirling on 4 April 1794. [SBR]

CHRISTIE, JOHN, was admitted as a burgess and guilds-brother of Stirling on 11 August 1797 [SBR]

CHRISTIE, ROBERT, was admitted as a burgess and guilds-brother of Stirling on 11 August 1797 [SBR]

CHRISTIE, WILLIAM, was admitted as a burgess and guilds-brother of Stirling on 2 October 1794. [SBR]

CHRISTIE, WILLIAM, was admitted as a burgess and guilds-brother of Stirling on 11 January 1797. [SBR]

CHRISTIE, WILLIAM, born 16 December 1817, son of John Christie and his wife Janet Jamieson in Kincardine on Forth, Clackmannanshire, died in Port of Spain, Trinidad, on 4 April 1838. [Tullialan gravestone]

CHRISTIE, WILLIAM, born 1828, was apprenticed to Alexander Grant, by 1841 he was a clockmaker at 36 Port Street, Stirling, died in 1908. [OSC.64]

CHRYSTAL, JAMES, the Procurator Fiscal for Stirling in 1835. [SJA.4/12,4B]

CHRYSTAL, ROBERT, born 1778, died at Park of Boqhan in April 1848, husband of Margaret Harvey, born 1791, died 4 April 1848. [Kippen gravestone, Stirlingshire]

CHRYSTAL, WILLIAM, born 1801 in Stirling, son of William Chrystal a schoolmaster in Glasgow, was educated at Glasgow University in 1814, died in Missouri in 1858. [MAGU]

CLARK, JOHN, from Bannockburn, Stirlingshire, died in Cincinatti, Ohio, on 18 October 1849. [SO]

CLARK, ROBERT, died in Chicago, Illinois, on 21 October 1852. [SO]

CLARK, THOMAS, died in Barbados on 12 January 1843. [SO]

CLARK, WILLIAM, master of the Neptune of Kincardine from Alloa bound for Belfast in 1815, [NRS.E504.2.13]; Greenock with passengers bound for Montreal, Quebec, in 1816. [NRS.E504.15.112]

CLARK, WILLIAM HUNTER, a weaver in Devonside, Tillicoultry, Stirlingshire, was accused of poaching in 1844. [NRS.AD14.44.390]

CLOAG, ALEXANDER, [died 1881], a builder, and his wife Jane Sinclair, [1825-1898], parents of William Cloag, born 1860, who was drowned in the Hudson River, New York, on 17 August 1886. [Greenside gravestone, Alloa, Clackmannanshire]

CLUB, ALEXANDER, was admitted as a burgess of Stirling on 24 December 1796. [SBR]

CLUGSTONE, WILLIAM, was admitted as a burgess and guilds-brother of Stirling on 12 July 1793. [SBR]

COATS, Mrs ELIZABETH, wife of George Coats formerly a merchant in St John, New Brunswick, died in Polmont near Falkirk, Stirlingshire, in December 1828. [New Brunswick Courier, 1.8.1829]

COATS, GEORGE, a merchant in St John, New Brunswick, and Elizabeth Esplin, daughter of John Esplin of Bowieshall, Stirlingshire, were married there on 27 July 1819. [NBC.11.9.1819]

COCKBURN, WILLIAM, married Agnes Laing, in Calcutta, India, 12 December 1844. [SO]

COLDSTREAM, JOHN, in Dunblane, a letter to Colonel Thomas Graham of Balgowan, 1798. [NRS.GD155.875]

COLLEN, HENRY, a slater from Doune, Stirlingshire, was admitted as a burgess of Dunfermline on 24 November 1786. [DM]

COLQUHOUN, ISABELLA, wife of James MacLay, [1828-1880], died in Brisbane, Queensland, Australia, on 7 July 1893. [St Ninian's gravestone, Stirling]

COLVIN, ALEXANDER, John Colvin, and Samuel Colvin, 1791. [Falkirk gravestone, Stirlingshire]

COLVIN, GEORGE, born 1760, died 21 May 1798, husband of Margaret Renny, born 1759, died 19 August 1838. [Falkirk gravestone, Stirlingshire]

CONNAL, JOHN, and his wife Helen Chrystall in the Mill of Cardross, parents of Janet Connal, born 1805, died 1824. [Kippen gravestone, Stirlingshire]

CONNAL, PATRICK, a banker in Stirling in 1828, [SJA. 14/8,1C]; agent of the National Bank of Scotland in Stirling in 1849. [POD]

COOPER, JOHN, a clockmaker in Stirling around 1826. [OSC.66]

COOPER, RICHARD, a clock and watch-maker in Falkirk from 1830 to 1840. [OSC.108]

COPLAND, JOHN, jr, a mariner in Kincardine, Tulliallan, testament, 1806, Comm. Dunblane. [NRS.CC6]

CORBETT, JAMES, a veterinary surgeon in Kilsyth, in 1838. [SJA.5/1.4D]

CORBET, WILLIAM, a maltman, was admitted as a burgess of Stirling on 19 November 1793. [SBR]

COUTT, GILBERT, master of the Friends of Kincardine trading between Alloa and Riga, Latvia, in 1817. [NRS.E504.2.13]

COVENTRY, THOMAS, found guilty of forgery, was sentenced to transportation to the colonies, at Stirling on 9 September 1811. [SM.83.10.790]

COWAN, JAMES, died in San Francisco, California, in April 1853. [SO]

COWAN, JOHN, a baker in Falkirk, Stirlingshire, married Margaret Leishman a daughter of James Leishman a carrier in Falkirk, later he abandoned her and went to America in 1786. [Process of Declarator of Marriage and Adherence, 1800, Commissariat of Edinburgh]. [NRS]

CRAIG, JAMES, a maltman, was admitted as a burgess and guildsbrother of Stirling on 7 October 1796. [SBR]

CRAIGIE, Captain, master of the <u>General Graham of Alloa</u> from Alloa, Clackmannanshire, with passengers bound for Quebec in 1834 and 1842, also with passengers bound for St John, New Brunswick, in 1847. [Quebec Mercury][St John Morning News]

CRANSTON, JAMES, in Doune in 1849. [SJA.9/11.4E]

CRAWFORD, DANIEL, master of the <u>Resolution of Alloa</u> from Greenock to Quebec in 1795. [NRS.E504.15.68]

CRAWFORD, GEORGE, a clock and watchmaker in Falkirk from 1830 until 1836. [OSC.108]

CRAWFORD, GEORGE, a merchant from Stirling, married Mary Ann Gosling, in Wellington, New Zealand, 18 June 1846. [SO]

CRAWFORD, JAMES, a tailor, was admitted as a burgess and guildsbrother of Stirling on 14 May 1793. [SBR]

CRAWFORD, JOHN, an author in Alloa, Clackmannanshire, in 1854. [SJA.16/6,3B]; born 1816, died 13 December 1873, father of Alexander Hope Crawford in Toronto, Ontario. [Alloa gravestone, Clackmannanshire]

CRAWFORD, JOHN, in Alva, Clackmannanshire, father of John James Crawford, born 1852, died in Semaphore, Adelaide, South Australia, on 2 December 1884. [S.12959]

CRAWFORD, JOHN, born 1831, a merchant and a banker, died at Craigmore, Rothesay, on 20 April 1878. [Alva gravestone, Clackmannanshire]

CRAWFORD, MARGARET, married George Steineth Harding from St Croix in the Danish West Indies, in Fairfield, Ayrshire, on 26 August 1811. [DPCA.476]; she died in St Croix in October 1835. [Logie gravestone, Stirlingshire]

CROMBIE, ANDREW CREACH, MD, born 1830, son of James Crombie in Culross, [1782-1857], and his wife Ruth ...., [1789-1874], died in Faisons, North Carolina, on 8 February 1864. [Dollar gravestone, Clackmannanshire]

CROMBIE, JAMES, born 1772, died at Culross on 2 March 1857, husband of Ruth ...., born 1789, died on 28 June 1874. [Dollar gravestone, Clackmannanshire]

CROSS, ANDREW, the Sheriff Substitute of Dunblane in 1839. [SJA.27/9.4D]

CULBERT, ALEXANDER, master of the Nelly and Ann of Stirling trading between Montrose, Angus, and Alloa, Clackmannanshire, in 1816. [NRS.E504.2.13]

CULBERT, DAVID, a mason and later of the Rob Roy Inn in Doune, Stirlingshire, Master of the Lodge St James number 171 from 1804 until 1805. [DHN.iii]

CUMMING, JAMES, master of the Dalmarnock of Alloa, trading between Greenock and Miramachi, New Brunswick, in 1820, and between Greenock and New York in 1826 and 1828, [NRS.E504.15.128/134]

CUMMINGS, Mr, a baker in Bannockburn, Stirlingshire, in 1857. [SJA.8/5,3D]

CUNNINGHAM, Sir DAVID, of Cambusmore in 1855. [SJA.26/10,3C]

CUNNINGHAM, JAMES, and J. McN., 1805. [Falkirk gravestone, Stirlingshire]

CUPPLES, GEORGE, minister of the Kilmadock Free Church, Doune, Stirlingshire, a petition, 1 May 1845. [NRS.GD112.51.189]

CURLE, or SLIGHT, Mrs MARGARET, from Bridge of Allan, Stirlingshire, died in Australia on 3 December 1859, inventory, testament 1861, Comm. Edinburgh. [NRS]

CURRER, ROBERT, born around 1809, a clock and watchmaker in Falkirk, Stirlingshire, from 1839 until 1876, died 1878. [SC.108]

CUTHILL, ARCHIBALD, Lieutenant of the Loyal Stirling Volunteers, was admitted as a burgess and guilds-brother of Dunfermline, Fife, on 17 July 1794. [DM]

CUTHEL, JAMES, and Agnes Drysdale, 1811. [Falkirk gravestone, Stirlingshire]

CUTHILL, ARCHIBALD, a Lieutenant of the Loyal Stirling Volunteers, was admitted as a burgess and guilds-brother of Dunfermline, Fife, on 17 July 1794. [DM]

CUTHILL, JAMES, in Denny, Stirlingshire, in 1857. [SJA.7/8.SA]

DALGLEISH, DAVID, was admitted as a burgess and guilds-brother of Stirling on 28 April 1797. [SBR]

DALGLEISH, ROBERT, a clock and watchmaker in Falkirk from 1805 until 1832. [OSC.108]

DALRYMPLE, HENRY, born 1800, died on 6 July 1866. [Alloa gravestone, Clackmannanshire]

DALZIEL, Mr, a banker in Falkirk, Stirlingshire, in 1855. [SJA.10/8.3C]

DANSKIN, JANET, spouse of John Brown a brewer in Stirling, testament, 1798, Comm. Stirling. [NRS]

DAREY, FRANCIS, born 1751 in France, died on 1 October 1839, husband of Elizabeth Morison, born in 1761, died on 15 August 1839. [Logie Old gravestone, Stirlingshire]

DAVIE, JAMES, a weaver, was admitted as a burgess of Stirling in 1804. [SBR]

DAVIE, RICHARD, a weaver, was admitted as a burgess of Stirling on 25 September 1791. [SBR]

DAWSON, ANDREW, born 1783 in Stirlingshire, participated in the Uprising of 1820, found guilty at Stirling of rebellion, was transported to New South Wales, Australia, in 1821, worked for the Government at around Sydney and by 1825 was Principal Overseer of Works at Newcastle, he was granted a Certificate of Freedom in 1827, he died at West Maitland on 15 April 1839. [TSR]

DAVIDSON, GEORGE, a skipper in Kincardine Tulliallan, testament, 12 October 1793, Comm. Dunblane. [NRS]

DAWSON, ELIZABETH, born 1802, daughter of William Dawson and his wife Ann Muirhead, died 31 October 1811. [Falkirk gravestone, Stirlingshire]

DAWSON, GEORGE, born 14 March 1813 in Falkirk, Stirlingshire, emigrated to America in 1818, a printer and journalist, died in Albany, New York State, on 17 February 1883. [WA]

DAWSON, JAMES, a manufacturer in Tillicoultry, Clackmannanshire, [sequestration, 1840. [NRS.CS280.15.5]

DAWSON, JAMES, a watchmaker in Port Street, Stirling, from 1845 until his death on 24 August 1863. [OSC.67]

DAWSON, JOHN, born 1819, postmaster at Blairlogie, died on 7 September 1906, husband of Janet Baird, born 1840, died in Bride of Allan on 14 February 1921. [Logie Old gravestone, Stirlingshire]

DAWSON, JOSEPH, born in Keswick on 7 May 1788, manager of the Carron Works in Falkirk, Stirlingshire, from 1825 until his death in Carron on 7 May 1850. [Larbert gravestone, Stirlingshire]; [SJA.18/1.4D]

DAWSON, MARGARET, second daughter of Robert Dawson in Alloa, Clackmannanshire, married Henry A. Oakman of Troy, New York, in South Brooklyn, Long Island, N.Y., on 20 March 1861. [S.1817]

DAWSON, PATRICK, of Campsie, Stirlingshire, in 1830. [SJA.22/4,4C]

DAWSON, PETER, born 1831, for 32 years was miller at Dunipace Mill, died 15 November 1909, husband of Isabella Dollar, born 1832, died 15 March 1909. [Falkirk gravestone, Stirlingshire]

DAWSON, PETER, a draper in Alloa, Clackmannanshire, in 1852. [SJA.9/4,4E]

DAWSON, ROBERT, a cordiner, was admitted as a burgess of Stirling on 18 February 1803. [SBR]

DAWSON, ROBERT, born 1838, son of John Dawson, died in Brucefield, Christchurch, New Zealand, on 23 August 1897. [Larbert Old gravestone, Stirlingshire]

DAWSON, WILLIAM, a manufacturer in Alva, Clackmannanshire, sequestration in 1844. [NRS.CS280.30.33]

DAWSON, WILLIAM, born 1814, for 34 years farm grieve of the Dunipace Estate, died 30 April 1886, husband of Agnes Muir, born 1835, died 20 February 1915. [Falkirk gravestone, Stirlingshire]

DEANS, ANDREW, in Stirling, in 1854. [SJA.17/3.3D]

DEMPSTER, GEORGE, a merchant in Montreal, Quebec, heir to his grandfather George Dempster, a baker in Alloa, Clackmannanshire, in 1848; also, heir to his mother Helen Duncan or Dempster in Alloa, in 1853. [NRS.S/H]

DEMPSTER, or DRYSDALE, HELEN, in Alva, Clackmannanshire, dead by 1850, mother of William Drysdale in Fremington, USA. [NRS.S/H]

DEMPSTER, Reverend JOHN, of Denny, Stirlingshire, 1823. [SJA.20/2]

DANIEL, DANIEL, a mechanic, was admitted as a burgess of Stirling on 27 September 1797. [SBR]

DEWAR, DAVID, a watch and clockmaker, son of James Dewar, Doune, Stirlingshire, Master of the Lodge St James number 171 from 1822-1823, also 1834-1835. [DHN.iii]

DEWAR, JAMES, son of Alexander Dewar of Severie, a mason and feuar in Doune, Stirlingshire, Master of the Lodge St James number 171, from 1814-1815. [DHN.iii]

DEWAR, PETER, a cordiner, was admitted as a burgess of Stirling on 17 January 1794 [SBR]

DEWAR, WILLIAM S., born 1798 in Tillicoultry, Clackmannanshire, second son of James Dewar in Cairnton Cottage, emigrated via Dundee on the brig Traveller of Aberdeen bound for Charleston, South Carolina, in 1822, a merchant, died there on 14 October 1848, [1849?]. [NARA][Old Scots gravestone, Charleston] [SG.18.1876] [SO]

DICK, GEORGE, a weaver, was admitted as a burgess of Stirling on 2 June 1794. [SBR]

DICK, GEORGE, and Jean Downie, 1798. [Falkirk gravestone, Stirlingshire]

DICK, JAMES, born 1802, farmer at Torrance, died 28 January 1884, husband of Jean Galbraith, born 1813, died 28 March 1891. [Kippen gravestone, Stirlingshire]

DICK, JOHN, sr., was admitted as a burgess and guilds-brother of Stirling on 1 November 1796. [SBR]

DICK, JOHN, a skipper in Bainsford, Falkirk, Stirlingshire, testament, October 1797, Comm. Stirling. [NRS]

DICK, JOHN, of Compston, a skipper in Bainsford, Stirlingshire, testament, 1805, Comm. Stirling. [NRS]

DICK, JOHN, III, a weaver, was admitted as a burgess of Stirling in 1804. [SBR]

DICK, JOHN, born 1826, an apprentice clockmaker in Stirling in 1841. [OSC.67]

DICK, ROBERT, a weaver, was admitted as a burgess of Stirling on 2 June 1794. [SBR]

DICK, ROBERT, was admitted as a burgess and guilds-brother of Stirling, on 14 June 1800. [SBR]

DICKSON, Reverend DAVID, in Bothkennar, Stirlingshire, was admitted as a burgess and guilds-brother of Dunfermline, Fife, on 6 June 1792. [DM]

DICKSON, EBENEZER, a weaver, was admitted as a burgess of Stirling on 6 October 1797. [SBR]

DICKSON, JAMES W., Sheriff Substitute of Stirlingshire, 1847. [SJA.18/6E]

DOBBIE, GEORGE, born 1828, a clock and watchmaker in Falkirk around 1852. [OSC.108]

DOBBIE, ROBERT, a mechanic, was admitted as a burgess of Stirling in 1804. [SBR]

DOBBIE, WILLIAM, born 1796, a clock and watchmaker in Falkirk from 1820 until 1845, watch and clockmaker to Queen Victoria, died in 1864. [OSC.108]

DODDS, THOMAS, was admitted as a burgess and guilds-brother of Stirling in 1807. [SBR]

DODS, THOMAS, with his wife Helen Maxwell, and eight sons, from Alloa, Clackmannanshire, emigrated to Canada on the David of London in 1821, settled in Lanark, Ontario, on 14 August 1821. [SG][PAO]

DOIG, PATRICK, born 1763, a physician and Colonel of the Militia in Antigua, died in Stirling on 9 May 1833. [Stirling gravestone]

DOLLAR, JAMES, born 1849 in Grahamston, Falkirk, Stirlingshire, son of William Dollar and his wife Mary Melville, dead in San Rafael, California, in March 1898. [Falkirk gravestone, Stirlingshire]

DOLLAR, WILLIAM, died in Ottawa, Canada, in 1873, was buried in Beechwood Cemetery. [Falkirk gravestone, Stirlingshire]

DONALD, JAMES, born in 1836, died at sea off South America on 29 November 1867. [Clackmannan gravestone]

DONALD, JOHN, a writer in Alloa, Clackmannanshire, in 1847. [SJA.9/44E]

DONALD, WILLIAM MCALISTER, married Georgina Moore, in Trieste, Italy, 30 June 1853. [SO]

DONALDSON, Mr, an artist in Stirling, 1827. [SAJ.15/2,1A]

DONNELLY, GEORGE, born 1832, of 20 Port Street, Stirling, was accused of theft and reset in 1852. [NRS.AD14.52.373]

DONNELLY, JOSEPH, born 1832, a weaver in Port Street, Stirling, was accused of theft and reset in 1852. [NRS.AD14.52.373]

DOUGAL, ARCHIBALD, a butcher was admitted as a burgess of Stirling in 1820. [SBR]

DOUGALL, JAMES, born 1758, farmer at Househill, died 23 June 1841, husband of Jean Marshal,

DOUGALL, JOHN, born 1798, a clock and watchmaker in Kippen around 1826 to 1836, died 1860. [OSC.109]

DOUGALL, JOHN, born 1773, died 14 February 1822. [Kippen gravestone, Stirlingshire]

DOUGLAS, ARCHIBALD, born in Stirling, died at 315 Dean Street, Brooklyn, New York, on 15 February 1863. [S.2450]

DOUGLAS, HENRY, a minister in Kilsyth, Stirlingshire, dead by 1850. [NRS.S/H]

DOUGLAS, JOHN, a weaver, was admitted as a burgess of Stirling on 25 July 1790 [SBR]

DOUGLAS, Captain ROBERT, a mariner, died in 1791. [Holy Rude gravestone, Stirling]

DOUGLAS, Captain ROBERT PERCY, married Anna Duckworth, in Berne, Switzerland, 10 December 1840. [SO]

DOUGLAS, ROBERT, a surgeon in Tobago, heir to his brother Henry Douglas, a minister in Kilsyth, Stirlingshire, in 1850. [NRS.S/H]

DOW, JAMES, of the Alloa Emigration Society, with his wife, three sons and four daughters, from Greenock aboard the David of London bound for Quebec, Canada, on 19 May 1821, was granted land in Lanark, Upper Canada on 14 August 1821. [PAO]

DOW, WALTER, a hammerman, was admitted as a burgess of Stirling in 1802. [SBR]

DOWNIE, ANDREW, a stabler in Stirling, testament, 1799, Comm. Stirling. [NRS]

DOWNIE, BENJAMIN, from Bellsdyke, Stirling, died in Clarendon, Jamaica, on 3 February 1794. [SM.56.118]

DOWNIE, CHRISTIAN, widow of Robert Willison a merchant in Stirling, testament, 1794, Comm. Stirling. [NRS]

DOWNIE, ROBERT, a maltman, was admitted as a burgess of Stirling on 20 September 1802. [SBR]

DOWNIE, ROBERT, a weaver, was admitted as a burgess of Stirling in 1804. [SBR]

DOWNIE, ROBERT, in Gargunnock, Stirlingshire, died 1 July 1865, father of Robert Thomson Downie, an agent in New York. [NRS.S/H]

DRUMMOND, Captain ARTHUR, of Cromlix, Stirlingshire,1856. [SJA.5/9,2C]

DRUMMOND, G.H. of Blair Drummond, Stirlingshire, 1834. [SJA.7/3,4C]

DRUMMOND, HENRY HOME, of Blair Drummond, Stirlingshire, an accounts book from 1820 until 1864. [NRS.GD24.1.811]

DRUMMOND, JOHN, born 1800 in Stirling, settled in Charleston, South Carolina, was naturalised there on 17 October 1825. [NARA.M1183.1]

DRUMMOND, NINIAN, a cordiner, was admitted as a burgess of Stirling on 14 April 1802. [SBR]

DRUMMOND, PETER, a seed merchant in Stirling, married Frances McBean, in Inverness, 13 June 1837. [SO]

DRUMMOND, ROBERT TURNBULL, born 1809, a goldsmith, jeweller and watchmaker at 9 Port Street, Stirling, from 1844 until his death in 1879. [OSC.71]

DRYSDALE, ANDREW, a hammerman, was admitted as a burgess of Stirling on 12 May 1798. [SBR]

DRYSDALE, ANDREW, in Stratford, Ontario, heir to his cousin James Taylor in Denny, Stirlingshire, who died on 18 March 1865. [NRS.S/H]

DRYSDALE, DAVID, in Tullibody, Clackmannanshire, a victim of theft and reset in 1852. [NRS.AD14.14.52.373]

DRYSDALE, JAMES, master of the Unity of Kincardine trading between Alloa and Riga, Latvia, in 1817. [NRS.E504.2.13]

DRYSDALE, JOHN, born 1842, died 29 March 1865 in Jefferson, St Louis, America. [Tillicoultry gravestone, Clackmannanshire]

DRYSDALE, WILLIAM, was admitted as a burgess and guilds-brother of Stirling in 1806. [SBR]

DRYSDALE, WILLIAM, a woollen manufacturer in Alva, Clackmannanshire, sequestration in 1843. [NRS.CS280.29.42]

DRYSDALE, WILLIAM, in Fremington, USA, son and heir of Helen Dempster or Drysdale in Alva, Stirlingshire, in 1850. [NRS.S/H]

DRYSDALE, Mrs, daughter of James Gibson in Clackmannanshire, and widow of Andrew Drysdale, a merchant in New York, married William Clark of London Street, Edinburgh, in Edinburgh on 22 November 1827. [EA.6679.759]

DUN, JAMES, was admitted as a burgess and guilds-brother of Stirling on 8 October 1796. [SBR]

DUNN, JOHN, a mechanic, was admitted as a burgess of Stirling on 30 October 1800. [SBR]

DUNBAR, HUGH, jr., a labourer in Neilston, Kilsyth, Stirlingshire. was accused of fraud in 1823. [NRS.AD14.23.126]

DUNCAN, GEORGE, a barber, was admitted as a burgess of Stirling on 12 November 1795. [SBR]

DUNCAN, GEORGE, a printer from Stirling, married Catherine Ferguson, in Adelaide, South Australia, on 19 October 1854. [SO]

DUNCAN, or DEMPSTER, HELEN, in Alloa, Clackmannanshire, dead by 1853, mother of George Dempster a merchant in Montreal, Quebec. [NRS.S/H]

DUNCAN, Dr THOMAS, from Glendevon, died in Aska, Genjam, India, on 1 October 1846. [SO]

DUNCANSON, JAMES, master of the Prince George of Alloa trading between Alloa and Miramachi, New Brunswick, in 1817. [NRS.E504.2.13]

DUNCANSON, ROBERT, master of the Morning Star of Alloa in 1819. [NRS.AD14.19.166]

DUNCANSON, ROBERT, in New York, son and heir of William Duncanson, a butcher in Stirling, in 1860. [NRS.S/H]

DUNCANSON, WILLIAM, a butcher in Stirling, dead by 1860, father of Robert Duncanson in New York. [NRS.S/H]

DUNDAS, JOSEPH, of Fingask and Carron Hall, born 26 November 1822, died on 7 July 1872, was buried at Monnetier, Haute Savoie, France. [Larbert gravestone, Stirlingshire]

DURANT, THOMAS and BENJAMIN DURANT, from Jamaica, apprentice millwrights in Alloa, Clackmannanshire, a deed subscribed in Alloa in 1790. [NRS.RD2.274.61]

DUTHIE, ARCHIBALD HAMILTON, a minister, was admitted as a burgess of Stirling in 1848. [SBR]

DUTHIE, JAMES, sometime in Jamaica, died in Stirling in 1817. [S.I.17]

EADIE, ANDREW, a mechanic, a burgess of Stirling in 1845. [SBR]

EADIE, GEORGE, a mason in Stirling, testament, 1791, Comm. Stirling. [NRS]

EADIE, JAMES, was admitted as a burgess and guilds-brother of Stirling in 1804. [SBR]

EADIE, JAMES, a tailor, was admitted as a burgess of Stirling in 1804. [SBR]

EADIE, JAMES, a wright in Ardoch, 1825. [SJA.21/7.4B]

EADIE, WILLIAM, born in Dunblane, Stirlingshire, son of Robert Eadie, [1760-1837], emigrated to Canada between 1815 and 1820. [SG]

EASTON, ANN, born 1763, niece of George Easton, died 24 February 1822. [Falkirk gravestone, Stirlingshire]

EASTON, ELIZABETH, born 1788, died 30 May 1816, wife of Adam Reid a calenderer in Glasgow. [Falkirk gravestone, Stirlingshire]

EDMOND, JAMES, was admitted as a burgess and guilds-brother of Stirling in 1804. [SBR]

EDMONSTONE, ARCHIBALD, in Stirling, died 28 January 1856, brother of William Edmonstone a merchant in Montreal, Quebec. [NRS.S/H]

EDMONSTONE, BETHIA, born 1798, daughter of Archibald Edmonstone of Spittal, [1754-1821], and his wife Elizabeth Aitken, [1762-1828], married John Montgomerie, died in Trinidad on 27 August 1821. [Stirling gravestone]

EDMONSTONE, CHARLES, born 1793, son of Archibald Edmonstone of Spittal, [1754-1821], and his wife Elizabeth Aitken, [1762-1828], died in Demerara on 1 September 1822. [Stirling gravestone]

EDMONSTONE, GEORGE, born 1795, son of Archibald Edmonstone of Spittal, [1754-1821], and his wife Elizabeth Aitken, [1762-1828], died in Demerara on 12 January 1818. [Stirling gravestone]

EDMONDSTONE, JOHN, third son of John Edmondstone in Cambuswallace, Stirlingshire, died in Jamaica on 10 November 1792. [SM.55.50]

EDMONSTONE, LOUISA HENRIETTA, second daughter of Sir Charles Edmonstone of Duntreath, Stirlingshire, married John Kingston of Clairmont, Demerara, in Hampton on 15 December 1829. [BM.27.549]

EDMONSTONE, WILLIAM, a merchant in Montreal, Quebec, brother and heir of Archibald Edmonstone in Stirling, who died on 28 January 1856. [NRS.SH]

EDWARD, CHRISTIAN, a schoolmistress in Stirling, a testament, 1791. Comm. Stirling. [NRS]

EGLINTON, JOHN, a maltman, was admitted as a burgess and guilds-brother of Stirling in 1813. [SBR]

ELDER, CHRISTIAN, born 1749, died in Denovan House on 2 May 1816, wife of George Easton. [Falkirk gravestone, Stirlingshire]

ELDER, WILLIAM, a maltman, was admitted as a burgess of Stirling in 1802. [SBR]

ELLIOT, MATTHEW, in Alva, Clackmannanshire, was a victim of theft and reset in 1852. [NRS.AD14.52.373]

ERSKINE, JAMES, born 1820, formerly a gas manager in Falkirk, Stirlingshire, died in St Kilda Road, South Melbourne, Australia, on 5 May 1885. [S.13085]

ERSKINE, JOHN THOMAS, Major of the Clackmannan Volunteers, was admitted as a burgess and guilds-brother of Dunfermline on 22 February 1804. [DM]

ESPLIN, ELIZABETH, youngest daughter of John Esplin of Bowieshall, Stirlingshire, married George Coats, a merchant in St John, New Brunswick, in Bowieshall on 27 July 1819. [NBC.11.9.1819]

EWING, EBENEZER, a merchant from Falkirk, Stirlingshire, who settled in Williamsburg, Virginia, by 1789. [NRS.CS17.1.8/348]

EWING, WILLIAM, born 1799, died 1877, and his wife Margaret Anderson, born 1806, died 1875, were parents of Archibald Ewing and Ralph Ewing who settled in Dunedin, New Zealand. [Logie gravestone, Stirling]

EWING, WILLIAM LECKIE, born 1802, died 1866 in Buxton, husband of Eleanor Mc Farlan, born 1802, died in Dollar, Clackmannanshire, in 1880, parents of Janet Buchanan Ewing, born 1835, died in Eaux Chaudes, France, in 1873, John Ewing born 1835, died in Manitoba in 1898. [Kippen gravestone, Stirlingshire]

EWING, WILLIAM, was admitted as a burgess and guilds-brother of Stirling in 1807. [SBR]

EWING, WILLIAM, a weaver, son of John Ewing, was admitted as a burgess of Stirling in 1850. [SBR]

FAIRBAIRN, JOHN, a nailer in Camelon, Stirlingshire, 1846. [SJA.14/4,4E]; 1856. [SO]

FAIRFUL, CHARLES, a soldier of the 42nd Highlanders, was appointed Drum Major of Stirling on 20 November 1856. [SO]

FAIRGRIEVE, ALEXANDER, in Falkirk, Stirlingshire, an appeal against suspension on 18 March 1843. [SO]

FAIRLIE, ANDREW, a butcher, was admitted as a burgess of Stirling in 1843, [CBR], in Stirling, died in hospital on 1 March 1855. [SO]

FARIE, GILBERT, a chemist in Bridge of Allan, Stirlingshire, 4 March 1852. [SO]

FARISH, JAMES, a merchant in Montreal, Quebec, married Jane Stevenson, in Wilton, 10 September 1840. [SO]

FENTON, JAMES, born 1848 in Dunfermline, Fife, a clockmaker in Stirling around 1871. [OSC.72]

FENTON, PETER, a cabinetmaker in Stirling, 5 July 1838. [SO]

FERGUS, DAVID, son of James Ferguson in Campsie, Stirlingshire, was educated at Glasgow University in 1779, a Relief Church minister in

Auchterarder, Perthshire, from 1787 until 1805, then in Campbeltown until 1822, emigrated to America, died in Cincinatti, Ohio. [MAGU]

FERGUSON, ALEXANDER, a manufacturer in Stirling, 20 September 1840. [SO]

FERGUSON, COLIN, the beadle of Stirling was appointed the Presbytery officer in 1844. [SO]

FERGUSON, Dr DANIEL, in Stirling, 1841. [SJA.30/4.4E]

FERGUSON, DANIEL, a shepherd from Stirlingshire, settled in Australia by 20 April 1854. [SO]

FERGUSON, DUNCAN, of the Balfron Emigration Society, Stirlingshire, with three daughters, from Greenock aboard the David of London bound for Quebec, Canada, on 19 May 1821, was granted land in Lanark, Upper Canada on 1 August 1821. [PAO]

FERGUSON, JAMES, a smith in Bridge of Allan, Stirlingshre, 1840. [SJA.24/1.4E]

FERGUSON, JAMES, born 1836, son of James Ferguson, [died 1853], and Mary Harvey, [died 1848], died in San Antonio, Texas, in 1866. [Holy Rude gravestone, Stirling]

FERGUSON, JOHN, son of A. Ferguson, a merchant in Falkirk, Stirlingshire, died in Kingston, Jamaica, on 11 April 1825. [S.578.421]

FERGUSON, JOHN, in High Street, Falkirk, Stirlingshire, a victim of theft and reset in 1852. [NRS.AD14.14.52.373]

FERGUSON, JOHN, son of James Ferguson, [died 1853], and Mary Harvey, [died 1848], settled in London, Canada. [Holy Rude gravestone, Stirling]

FERGUSON, PETER, born 1795, a labourer from Stirling, emigrated via Port Glasgow aboard the Favourite of St John bound for St John, New Brunswick, on 22 October 1815. [PANB.ms.RS23E.fo.9798]

FERGUSON, PETER, from Bridge of Teith, a divinity student in 1824, a minister in Canada. [AUPC]

FIFE, ALISON, in Square Row, Holton, Alloa, Clackmannanshire, was found guilty of the murder of his son Alison Fife, and was sentenced by the High Court in Edinburgh in 1844 to 14 years transportation to the colonies. [NRS.JC26.1844.471] [SO]

FINDLAY, JOHN, in Akron, Ohio, son and heir of Robert Findlay, a smith in Falkirk, Stirlingshire, died on 4 December 1873. [NRS.S/H]

FINLAYSON, CHRISTOPHER, a farmer in Dunblane, 15 July 1841. [SO]

FINLAYSON, JAMES, of Harperstoa in Stirling on 4 November 1847. [SO]

FISHBICK, THOMAS, from Alloa, Clackmannanshire, was admitted as a burgess and guilds-brother of Dunfermline on 19 November 1792. [DM]

FISHER, ROBERT, a teacher at Taylor's Institution, Crieff, on 29 March 1849. [SO]

FLEMING, JAMES, born 1818 in Falkirk, Stirlingshire, died in St John, New Brunswick, on 26 September 1875. [EC.28133]

FLEMING, JOHN, a schoolboy at the Ragged School in Stirling, was reported missing on 11 July 1855. [SO]

FLEMING, MALCOLM, and Janet Freeland, 1793. [Falkirk gravestone, Stirlingshire]

FLYN, Lieutenant Colonel JOHN, was admitted as a burgess and guilds-brother of Stirling in 1818. [SBR]

FOGGO, WILLIAM, was admitted as a burgess and guilds-brother of Stirling in 1804. [SBR]

FORBES, ALEXANDER, born 1793, son of Arthur Forbes, [1753-1831], a Major of the 79th Highlanders, died in Kingston, Upper Canada, on 30 March 1851. [Stirling gravestone]

FORBES, ARTHUR, born 1753, late of the North Carolina Highlanders, died in Stirling on 23 April 1831. [Stirling gravestone]

FORBES, CAMPBELL, born 1809, son of Arthur Forbes and his wife Jessie Campbell, died in Maneiro, Sydney, New South Wales, Australia, on 19 May 1844. [Holy Rude gravestone, Stirling]

FORBES, JESSY, daughter of Dugald Forbes, married Lieutenant Jacob Glyner Rogers of the 77th Regiment, at Melville Place, Stirling, on 24 September 1822. [SM.90.520]

FORDYCE, JOHN, a mechanic, was admitted as a burgess of Stirling in 1810. [SBR]

FORMAN, GEORGE, was admitted as a burgess and guilds-brother of Stirling in 1821. [SBR]

FORREST, DAVID, born 1827, son of John Forrest, [1792-1865], a merchant in Alloa, Clackmannanshire, and his wife Agnes Hay, [1799-1874], died in New York on 27 October 1859. [East Preston Street gravestone, Edinburgh]

FORREST, JAMES, from Stirling, a physician at Ochil Farm, Lake Wilson, Minnesota, testament, 1888. [NRS.SC70.1.268]

FORRESTER, ALEXANDER, a writer in Stirling, died in 1812, his wife Elizabeth MacEwan, died in 1805, their son John Forrester, a writer in Stirling, died in 1813, buried in Stirling. [St Cuthbert's gravestone, Edinburgh]

FORRESTER, ALEXANDER, a miller in Alloa, Clackmannanshire, a bankrupt, papers, 1826-1832. [NRS.CS96.4620]

FORRESTER, HELEN, of Polder, died 2 March 1833 in Helensfield, Kippen. [Kippen gravestone, Stirlingshire]

FORRESTER, JOHN, formerly in Braes, later in Stirling, testament, 1798, Comm. Stirling. [NRS]

FORRESTER, MURDOCH, born 1816, died in Oamaru, Otago, New Zealand, on 16 June 1881. [Gargunnock gravestone, Stirlingshire].

FORRESTER, Captain, master of the Charlotte of Alloa when bound for New Zealand struck a rock off Madeira on 18 April 1840, passengers and crew saved. [EEC.20222]

FOSSIT, SOLOMON, was admitted as a burgess and guilds-brother of Stirling in 1803. [SBR]

FOTHERINGHAM, ANN, in Alloa, Clackmannanshire, versus James Murray, a millwright or engineer, a Process of Divorce in 1810. [NRS.CC8.6.1395]

FOTHERINGHAM, ROBERT, a manufacturer in Tillicoultry, Clackmannanshire, a report, 13 November 1845. [SO]

FOTHERINGHAM, ..., agent of the Western Bank of Scotland in Alloa, Clackmannanshire, in 1849. [POD]

FOX, GEORGE, in Stirling, a soldier of the 42nd Highlanders, the Black Watch, was decorated on 24 May 1855 for services in Crimea. [SO]

FOYER, ARCHIBALD, a grazier at Knowhead, father of David Muir Foyer, born 1862, died in Sutherland, Nebraska, on 8 December 1914. [Campsie gravestone, Stirlingshire]

FOYER, DAVID, and his wife Christina Muir, were parents of Archibald Edmonston Foyer, born 186, died in Sumner, Nebraska, in February 1907, and William Foyer, born 1869, died in Sutherland, Nebraska, on 10 September 1895. [Campsie gravestone, Stirlingshire]

FRAME, JAMES, born 1766, eldest son of Reverend James Frame in Alloa, Clackmannanshire, settled in Blandford, Virginia, died in Petersburg, Va., on 26 October 1803. [DPCA.74] [AJ.2921]

FRAME, JAMES, a woodcutter in Touch, drowned at Cambuskenneth, Stirlingshire, on 26 January 1843. [SO]

FRANCE, ARCHIBALD, a smith and agricultural implement maker in Stirling, 6 September 1849.]SO]

FRANCE, JOHN, born in Buchlyvie, Stirlingshire, son of Reverend John France, was educated at Glasgow University in 1795, a Secession minister in Kirriemuir, Angus, from 1810 to 1816, later at Glade Run, Butler County, USA, from 1820 until 1841, died in 1861. [MAGU] [UPC]

FRANCE, ROBERT, born in 1820, died on 9 October 1896, husband of Jane Robertson, born 1824, died on 5 June 1892. [Logie Old gravestone, Stirlingshire]

FRASER, ALEXANDER, a shoemaker in Stirling, was elected 1st Lieutenant of the High Constables, on 1 January 1846. [SO]

FRASER, Mrs, in Stirling, 1840. [SJA.27/3,1B]

FRASER, ISABELLA, born 1777, died in Alloa in 1833, wife of John McCart in New Orleans. [Alloa gravestone, Clackmannanshire]

FRASER, JOHN, Sheriff Substitute of Stirling, 1824. [SJA.30/12,4C]

FRASER, JOHN, Captain of the Stirlingshire Militia, died 17 February 1853. [SO]

FRASER, RODERICK, a labourer in Stirling, testament, 1792, Comm. Stirling. [NRS]

FRASER, WILLIAM, born 1780, minister of the West United Presbyterian congregation, died on 3 September 1853. [Alloa gravestone, Clackmannanshire]

FRENCH, ANNE, wife of James Todd, in New York, died at Villafield, 23 July 1840. [SO]

FRENCH, LUCIUS, was admitted as a burgess and guilds-brother of Stirling in 1822. [SBR]

GALBRAITH, JOHN, 1770-1806, a watch and clockmaker in Falkirk. [OSC.108]

GALLOWAY, DAVID, born 1814, a skipper, died 27 September 1894, husband of Isabella Watson, born 1815, died 20 October 1890. [Alloa gravestone, Clackmannanshire]

GALLOWAY, JAMES, 'the parochial schoolmaster from 1754 till he died in 1816', husband of Margaret Suter, born 1772, died on 29

September 1854. [Logie Old gravestone, Stirlingshire]

GALLOWAY, JOHN, born 1815, a baker, 'late in New York', died on 31 January 1852, [Buchlyvie gravestone, Stirlingshire]

GALLOWAY, ROBERT, in Campsie, Stirlingshire, was murdered by his wife, 19 September 1844. [SO]

GARDENER, PETER, a blacksmith on the Shore, Stirling, 9 October 1851. [[SO]

GARDINER, Mr, a cooper in Stirling, 1857. [SJA.13/2,2C]

GARDNER, JOHN, was elected Master of the Coopers of Stirling, 30 September 1841. [SO]

GARDNER, WILLIAM, born 1742 in Drymen, Stirlingshire, settled in Jamaica in 1765, died in Kingston, Jamaica, on 28 December 1820. [DPCA][EA]

GEDDES, Mr, of Bannockburn Colliery, Stirlingshire, 1838. [SJA.21/12,4E]

GENTLE, ANDREW, a brewer in Dunblane, Stirlingshire, settled in Hemingford, Quebec, in 1801. [SC]

GENTLEMAN, EBENEZER, a writer in Stirling, 1855. [SJA.23/2.1B]

GIBSON, J., agent of the Edinburgh and Glasgow Bank in Dollar, Clackmannanshire, in 1849. [POD]

GALBRAITH, GEORGE, born 1801, settled in Narriga, New South Wales, Australia, died in Sydney, New South Wales, on 28 October 1838, buried there in St George's churchyard. [Kippen gravestone, Stirlingshire]

GALLOWAY, JOHN, a banker in New York, died in Buchlyvie, Kippen, Stirlingshire, in January 1852, testament, 1852. [NRS.SC70.1.77]

GALLOWAY, WILLIAM, son of Henry Galloway a merchant in Stirling, was apprenticed to Allan and Stewart, bankers in Edinburgh, for seven years on 23 February 1797. [ERA]

GALT, ALEXANDER, messenger at arms, Alloa, Clackmannanshire, 1849. [POD]

GARDNER, ALEXANDER, born 1804, died on 14 July 1851, husband of Janet Davie, born 1798, died on 22 June 1844. [Larbert gravestone, Stirlingshire]

GARDNER, ALEXANDER, born 1730, a smith in Stenhousemuir, died on 4 December 1804, husband of Margaret Henry, born 1731, died 25 December 1785. [Larbert gravestone, Stirlingshire]

GARDNER, JAMES, born 1804, died on 14 July 1851, husband of Janet Davie, born 1798, died 22 June 1844. [Larbert gravestone, Stirlingshire]

GARDNER, JAMES, born in 1824, a cooper in Stirling, died on 29 October 1883, husband of Jeannie McGregor, born in 1826, died on 10 May 1878. [Logie Old gravestone, Stirlingshire]

GARDNER, JOHN, a seaman in Grangemouth, Stirlingshire, an inventory, 1819, Comm. Stirling. [NRS]

GARDNER, WILLIAM, born 1742 in Drymen, Stirlingshire, settled in Jamaica in 1764, died in Kingston on 28 December 1820. [EEC.17132][EA][DPCA][S.5.218]

GENTLES, JOHN, and J.M., 1810. [Falkirk gravestone, Stirlingshire]

GIBB, JAMES, a watch and clockmaker in Stirling from 1770 until 1804. [OSC.73]

GIBB, JOHN, master of the Margaret of Kincardine trading between Hamburg, Germany, and Alloa in 1815. [NRS.E504.2.13]

GIBSON, JAMES, son of Peter Gibson a clock and watchmaker in Falkirk, Stirlingshire, was apprenticed to James Howden, a clock and watchmaker in Edinburgh, for seven years on 14 February 1793. [ERA]

GIBSON, SARAH, born 10 March 1807, daughter of James Gibson and his wife Mary Wilson in Dollar, Clackmannanshire, died in Tobago on 9 June 1902. [Dollar gravestone]

GILCHRIST, JOHN, Provost of Stirling in 1797. [NRS.B34.20.92]

GILCHRIST, JOHN, a clock and watchmaker in Kilsyth around 1820. [OSC.109]

GILLESPIE, THOMAS, from Stirlingshire, emigrated to America in 1817, was naturalised in New York on 12 October 1830. [NARA]

GILLESPIE, WILLIAM, son of William Gillespie a miller at Bridge of Allan, Stirlingshire, was apprenticed to Robert Lucas, a merchant in Edinburgh, for four years on 21 October 1799. [ERA]

GILLIES, J., a clock and watchmaker in Kilsyth around 1820. [OSC.109]

GILLIES, WILLIAM, in Roughmite, Denny, Stirlingshire, a victim of cattle theft in 1837. [NRS.AD14.37.528]

GLAS, ROBERT, born 1786, son of Provost Glas of Stirling, died in Belmont, Jamaica, in 1804. [AJ.2945][SM.66.479]

GLAS, WALTER STIRLING, Captain of the Loyal Stirling Volunteers, was admitted as a burgess and guilds-brother of Dunfermline, Fife, on 17 July 1804 [DM]

GLAS, WILLIAM BRYCE, born 1806, sixth son of John Glas in Stirling, died on St Toolies Estate, Jamaica, on 16 January 1825. [AJ.4032] [BM.17.760] [EA]

GOLDIE, PETER, son of James Goldie and his wife Helen Taylor, died in Milwaukee, Wisconsin, on 10 March 1859. [Campsie gravestone, Stirlingshire]

GOLDIE, ROBERT, son of James Goldie and his wife Helen Taylor, died in Sioux City, Iowa, on 31 March 1876. [Campsie gravestone, Stirlingshire]

GORDON, HUGH, eldest son of Captain Robert Gordon of Invercarron, died in Demerara on 8 September 1827. [EA.6671.703]

GORDON, Reverend THOMAS, in Falkirk, Stirlingshire, married Janet Connal, daughter of Reverend Patrick Connal of Bathgate, in Stirling on 17 September 1822. [SM.90.519]

GORDON, WILLIAM, son of John Gordon in Carron, Stirlingshire, nephew and heir of Lieutenant William McDonald of the 79th Regiment in Jamaica, 1797. [NRS.S/H]

GOSFORD, Mr, a dancing teacher in Alloa in 1840. [SJA.14/8,4F]

GOURLAY, JANET, in Stirling, relict of James Arthur a surgeon in the Royal Navy, testament, 22 December 1797, Comm. Stirling. [NRS]

GOURLAY, ROBERT, and Margaret Johnston, 1793. [Falkirk gravestone, Stirlingshire]

GRAHAM, CATHERINE MARGARET, married Captain James Briggs, at the Cape of Good Hope, South Africa, 10 September 1840. [SO]

GRAHAM, JAMES, from Falkirk, Stirlingshire, a minister in Charleston, South Carolina, 14 January 1790. [NRS.CS17.1.9/4]

GRAHAM, JAMES, a maltster and corn merchant in Alloa, Clackmannanshire, a sequestration in 1826. [NRS.CS236.G27.4]

GRAHAM, JAMES, of Buchlyvie, Stirlingshire, a feu contract with Thomas Lockhart, registered 10 December 1841. [NRS.RD29.3.23; vol.673.303]

GRAHAM, JOHN, of Meiklewood, 1826. [SJA.31/8.81c]

GRAHAM, JOHN, a draper in Rhode Island, heir to Janet Sneddon in Lauriston, Falkirk, Stirlingshire, 1852. [NRS.S/H]

GRAHAM, JOHN, born 1806, a licentiate of the Church of Scotland for 35 years an elder of the parish, and for 20 years inspector of the poor, died in 1870. [Kippen gravestone, Stirlingshire]

GRAHAM, MARGARET, born 1783, widow of John Carmichael a labourer in Doune, Stirlingshire, was accused of theft in 1840. [NRS.AD14.40.27]

GRAHAM, Reverend PATRICK, in Aberfoyle, Stirlingshire, letters, 1809-1812. [NRS.GD22.3.342-344

GRAHAM, ROBERT, mariner in Bothkennar, Stirlingshire, an inventory, 1823, Comm. Stirling. [NRS]

GRAHAM, ROBERT, born 1821, a carter in Craigneuch, Aberfoyle, Stirlingshire, was accused of forgery in 1851. [NRS.AD14.51.522]

GRAHAM, WILLIAM, in Gartmore, Stirlingshire, a Bond of Providence for his children, registered 5 July 1841, [NRS.RD29.3.23]; a victim of forgery, 1851. [NRS.AD14.51.522]

GRAHAM, WILLIAM CUNNINGHAM, of Gartmore, Stirlingshire, granted a tack or lease to James Partane, maltman of Garnculloch near Buchlyvie, Stirlingshire, on 20 January 1810. [NRS.GD22.1.510]

GRANT, ALEXANDER, born 17 February 1796, apprenticed to Henry Redpath, a clockmaker at 1 Bow Street, Stirling, from1824 until his death on 26 June 1875. [OSC.74] [Holy Rude gravestone, Stirling]

GRANT, GEORGE, in Stirling, 1845. [SJA.18/4,44G]

GRANT, JAMES W., born 1846, son of James Grant a coach proprietor and hotelkeeper in Stirling, died on Broadway, New York, on 8 April,

GRANT, PETER, of the Established Ragged School in Stirling in 1853. [SJA.25/2.4D]

GRAY, JAMES, a clock and watchmaker in Balfron, Stirlingshire, around 1850. [OSC.108]

GRAY, MARY, in Stirling, niece and heir of John Paton in Jamaica, in 1832. [NRS.S/H]

GRAY, THOMAS, shipmaster in Kincardine, testament, 1821, Comm. Dunbarton. [NRS.CC10.29.269]

GRAY, Mr, a dancing teacher in Falkirk, Stirlingshire, in 1830. [SJA.21/10,4C]

GREEN, HUGH, in Falkirk, Stirlingshire, 1834. [SJA.10/10,4E]

GREEN, JAMES, and I. McGilligan, 1811. [Falkirk gravestone, Stirlingshire]

GREIG, WILLIAM, a vagrant beggar from Alloa, Clackmannanshire, then imprisoned in Stirling, accused of housebreaking in 1819. [NRS.AD14.19.88]

GRINDLAY, JOHN, messenger at arms, Falkirk, Stirlingshire, 1849. [POD]; 1840. [SJA.23/10, 1A]

GUACK, MATTHEW, a former Lieutenant of the 10th Stirlingshire Militia, with his family, settled in Ramsay, Upper Canada, on 13 April 1821. [PAO]

HAIG, CALDOM, daughter of John Haig a merchant in Alloa, Clackmannanshire, married James Miller, a merchant in Charleston, South Carolina, in Edinburgh on 18 July 1799. [Edinburgh OPR]

HALDANE, JAMES, was admitted as a burgess and guilds-brother of Stirling in 1808. [SBR]

HALL, FRANCIS, in Clackmannan, applied to settle in Canada in 1818. [TNA.CO384.3]

HALL, JAMES, and family, from Clackmannanshire, emigrated to Canada in 1820, settled in Lanark, Ontario. [BNA]

HALL, JOHN, in Clackmannan, applied to settle in Canada in 1818. [TNA.CO384.3]

HALLY, GEORGE, a farmer in Torwood, Stirlingshire, brother and heir of Charles Hally in Maine, 1840. [NRS.S/H]

HAMILTON, ALEXANDER, born 1805, died in Tasmania, Australia, on 9 July 1884. [Holy Rude gravestone, Stirling]

HAMILTON, JAMES, late in Jamaica, later in Falkirk, Stirlingshire, testament, 8 November 1796, Comm. Stirling. [NRS]

HAMILTON, JOHN BUCHANAN, of Leny and Aberdowie, Stirlingshire, 1847. [SJA.27/8,4E]

HAMILTON, Captain, master of the Retreat of Alloa from Alloa, Clackmannanshire, with passengers bound for Quebec in 1852.

HANDYSIDE, ROBERT, the Sheriff of Stirling in 1840. [SJA.17/7,4E]

HANNA, JOHN, was admitted as a burgess and guilds-brother of Stirling in 1809. [SBR]

HANTON, JOHN, an engineer in Alloa in 1842. [SJA.25/11,4E]

HARDIE, DAVID, born 1813, son of James Hardie and his wife Janet Kincaid, 'late of Victoria, Australia', died on 8 February 1852. [Falkirk gravestone, Stirlingshire]

HARDIE, JOHN, an inventor in Stirling in 1859. [SJA.10/6,4C]

HARDIE, THOMAS, a Lieutenant of the Loyal Stirling Volunteers, was admitted as a burgess and guilds-brother of Dunfermline, Fife, on 17 July 1804. [DM]

HARDIE, THOMAS, married Jane Clark, in Melbourne, Australia, on 2 December 1852. [SO]

HARLEY, ARCHIBALD, tollkeeper at Beancross, Falkirk, Stirlingshire, dead by 1855, father of Alexander Harley in USA. [NRS.S/H]

HARLEY, CHARLES, a merchant in Alloa, Clackmannanshire, disposed of a tenement in Alloa to John Francis Erskine of Mar in 1795. [NRS.GD124.1.880]

HARROWER, JAMES, was found guilty of the murder of Margaret, wife of Robert Hunter of Fisheross, Clackmannanshire, in 1840, trial papers, [NRS.JC26.1840.215]

HARVIE, ALEXANDER, a baker in Stirling, testament, 1791, Comm. Stirling. [NRS]

HARVEY, ALEXANDER, born 1747, a farmer from Stirlingshire, agent of the Arnprior Society of Emigrants, established a settlement in Barnet, Caledonia County, Vermont in 1775, died there, a landowner, judge, and militia colonel, on 14 December 1800. [West Barnet gravestone]

HARVIE, GEORGE, born 1760, farmer at Shirgarton, died 1 August 1841, husband of Helen Shirra, born 1761, died 2 August 1852. [Kippen gravestone, Stirlingshire]

HARVEY, GEORGE, born 1771, son of John Harvey a wright in

Glentiranmuir, Kippen, was apprenticed to David Somerville in 1771, a clockmaker in St Ninian's from 1795 to 1806, and in Stirling from 1806 until his death in August 1835. [OC.76][St Ninian's gravestone, Stirlingshire]

HARVIE, GEORGE, an artist in Stirling in 1863. [SJA.23/2,4B]

HARVEY, ROBERT, a surgeon in Stirling, died 24 May 1867, father of Archibald Harvey in Bombay, India. [NRS.S/H]

HARVEY, WILLIAM, born 1807, son of George Harvey, a watch and clockmaker in Stirling from 1834 until his death in 1883. [OSC.76]

HARVIE-BROWN, ALEXANDER, of Dunipace, born 27 August 1844, died 26 July 1916. [Falkirk gravestone, Stirlingshire]

HARVIE-BROWN, JOHN, born in June 1801, died in October 1880, husband of Elizabeth....., born 14 May 1807, died 7 June 1888. . [Falkirk gravestone, Stirlingshire]

HAWLEY, or HENDERSON, ISOBELLA, in New York, heir to her grandfather Daniel Manson, a schoolmaster in Stirling, in 1834. [NRS.S/H]

HAY, DAVID, Major of the Loyal Stirling Volunteers, was admitted as a burgess and guilds-brother of Dunfermline on 17 July 1804. [DM]

HAY, JAMES, a weaver, was admitted as a burgess of Stirling in 1854. [SBR]

HAY, ROBERT, born 1838, late of the North British American Bank in Montreal, Quebec, died in Denny, Stirlingshire, 'after a long lingering illness'. [DA.1773]

HEALEY, JOSEPH, was admitted as a burgess and guilds-brother of Stirling in 1852. [SBR]

HEMPSEED, WILLIAM, was admitted as a burgess and guilds-brother of Stirling in 1806. [SBR]

HENDERSON, DAVID, in Alva, Clackmannanshire, a victim of theft in Stirling in 1837. [NRS.AD14.37.207]

HENDERSON, or SNYDER, ELIZABETH, in New York, heir to her grandfather Daniel Manson a schoolmaster in Stirling, 1834. [NRS.S/H]

HENDERSON, or HAWLEY, ISOBELLA, in New York, heir to her grandfather Daniel Manson a schoolmaster in Stirling, 1834. [NRS.S/H]

HENDERSON, J., an iron merchant in Stirling in 1835. [SJA.11/12,4B]

HENDERSON, JAMES, of Rosebank, writer in Falkirk, Stirlingshire, dead by 1818, father of Peter Henderson in St John, Newfoundland. [NRS.S/H]

HENDERSON, JAMES, of Springfield, born 1765, died on 21 July 1832, father of William Henderson, born 1798, a merchant in Santiago, Chile, died on 15 September 1825. [Larbert gravestone, Stirlingshire]

HENDERSON, or ROACH, JANE, in New York, heir to her grandfather Daniel Manson a schoolmaster in Stirling, 1834. [NRS.S/H]

HENDERSON, JESSIE, born on 4 November 1828 in Gibraltar, died in Dollar on 12 March 1846. [Dollar gravestone, Clackmannanshire]

HENDERSON, JOHN, a manufacturer in Tillicoultry, Stirlingshire, sequestration, 1840. [NRS.CS280.26.25]

HENDERSON, JOHN, a weaver in Cambusbarron, Stirlingshire, died 14 July 1841, father of Robert Henderson in Beckwith, Canada West. [NRS.S/H]

HENDERSON, JOHN, born 1791, a butcher in Alloa, died on 30 January 1850, husband of Mary Maule, who died on 14 April 1867. [Alva gravestone, Clackmannanshire]

HENDERSON, MARY ANN, daughter of James Henderson of Springfield, Stirlingshire, married Reverend A. M. Wordie of the Scots Kirk, in Kingston, Jamaica, on 4 December 1826. [BM.21.772]

HENDERSON, MATTHEW, born 1831, son of John Henderson and his wife Janet Lennox, died in Melbourne, Australia, on 9 August 1877. [Logie gravestone, Stirling]

HENDERSON, PETER, in St John's, Newfoundland, grandson and heir of Robina Henderson or MacCraire in Falkirk, Stirlingshire, 1819. [NRS.S/H]

HENDERSON, PETER, son of James Henderson of Rosebank, [1781-1848], and his wife Katherine Wyse, a merchant in St John's, Newfoundland, died in Rosebank on 18 April 1826. [Falkirk gravestone, Stirlingshire]; son and heir of James Henderson, a writer in Falkirk, in 1820. [NRS.S/H]

HENDERSON, ROBERT, a weaver, was admitted as a burgess of Stirling in 1802. [SBR]

HENDERSON, ROBERT, was found guilty of assault and sentenced in Stirling to seven years transportation to the colonies in 1815. [NRS.GD1.959]

HENDERSON, ROBERT, in Carlton Place, Beckwith, Canada West, son and heir of John Henderson a weaver in Cambusbarron, Stirlingshire, who died on 14 July 1841. [NRS.S/H]

HENDERSON, THOMAS, born 1783, a baker, died 17 May 1831, husband of Helen Kirkcaldie, born 1788, died 25 June 1875. [Alloa gravestone, Clackmannanshire]

HENDERSON, WILLIAM, born 1808, 'upwards of twenty years in the service of the Royal Oak Hotel in Alloa, Clackmannanshire,' died in Sydney, New South Wales, Australia, on 1 December 1884. [S.12963]

HENRY, Mr, a merchant in Crieff in 1839. [SJA.29/3.4F]

HERON, GEORGE, in Detroit, Michigan, heir to William Simpson, a nurseryman in Falkirk, Stirlingshire, who died on 19 October 1850. [NRS.S/H]

HEUGH, ANDREW, a planter in Montgomery County, Maryland, died 6 January 1771, son of Thomas Heugh a merchant in Falkirk, Stirlingshire, testament 22 June 1791. [NRS.CC8.8.126]

HEUGH, JOHN, in Montgomery County, Maryland, eldest son of Andrew Heugh of Leek Forest, Montgomery County, Maryland, a deed subscribed in 1789, refers to his grandfather Thomas Heugh, a merchant in Falkirk, Stirlingshire, and to Charles Heugh, his second son, also to property in Baxter's Wynd, Falkirk. [NRS.RD2.252.1227]

HEUGH, JOHN, born 1813, son of Walter Heugh, [1776-1854], and his wife Janet Bald, [1787-1837], died in Nevada City, USA, on 21 August 1867. [Airth gravestone. Stirlingshire]

HEUGH, WALTER, born 1816, son of Walter Heugh, [1776-1854], and his wife Janet Bald, [1787-1837], died in Philadelphia, Pennsylvania, on 31 July 1857. [Airth gravestone. Stirlingshire]

HEUGH, WILLIAM, born 1811, son of Walter Heugh, [1776-1854], and his wife Janet Bald, [1787-1837], died in Nevada City, USA, on 21 August 1867. [Airth gravestone. Stirlingshire]

HEWIT, ALEXANDER, a tailor, was admitted as a burgess of Stirling in 1816. [SBR]

HILL, C. THOROLD, a Captain of the 29th Regiment, married Emma Harriot, Russell, in Stirling, 5 September 1844. [SO]

HILL, or HILLOCK, THOMAS, a weaver in Alloa, Clackmannanshire, and his wife Janet Naismith, disposed of property in Alloa to John Francis Erskine of Mar in 1801. [NRS.GD124.1.887]

HISLOP, ROBERT, a post runner between Dollar and Glendevon in 1858. [SJA.9/4,5D]

HISLOP, THOMAS, a minister in Doune, Stirlingshire, a letter in June 1844; a petition in May 1845. [NRS.GD112.74.827; GD112.51.195]

HODGE, DAVID, son of J. Hodge a Customs Officer at Alloa, Clackmannanshire, a planter in Jamaica in 1829. [NNQ.IV.137]

HODGE, Mrs H., a hotelier in Stirling in 1853. [SJA.11/2, 24E]

HODGE, THOMAS, a weaver, was admitted as a burgess and guilds-brother of Stirling in 1804. [SBR]

HOGG, JAMES, born in 1791, died in Grangemouth in 1821, husband of Jane Jack, born in 1793, died at Powmill, Airth Road, on 16 December 1872. [Muiravonside gravestone, Stirlingshire]

HOG, GEORGE, a shipmaster in Clackmannan, inventory, 1810, Comm. Stirling. [NRS]

HOGG, JOHN, born in 1830, a master mariner, died in Brisbane, Australia, in 1884. [Dollar gravestone, Clackmannanshire]

HOGG, Captain JOSEPH, died in Quebec on 13 June 1866. [Polmont gravestone, Stirlingshire]

HOGGAN, Dr, a surgeon in Denny, Stirlingshire, in 1857. [SJA.16/10,3A]

HOLMAN, THOMAS, was admitted as a burgess and guilds-brother of Stirling in 1807. [SBR]

HOLMAN, SAMUEL, son of Thomas Holman, was admitted as a burgess and guilds-brother of Stirling in 1842. [SBR]

HORN, ..., and his wife Jean Shirer, parents of Jean Horn, born 1851, widow of William MacAlister in Pittsburgh, Pennsylvania, died there on 2 November 1912. [Baldernock gravestone, Stirlingshire]

HONEYMAN, ALEXANDER, born 25 November 1800, died on 22 May 1861, husband of Christina Bauld, born 17 October 1802, died on 17 October 1874, parents of John Honeyman, who died in Agra, United Provinces, India, aged 30. [Larbert gravestone, Stirlingshire]

HORN, WILLIAM, in Carronvale near Falkirk in 1840. [SJA.27/3,3F]

HOSIE, WILLIAM, a shipowner on Stirling Shore, was admitted as a burgess and guilds-brother of Stirling in 1819. [SBR]

HOTCHKIES, CORNELIUS, in Carronshore, born 1832, died on 6 March 1851. [Larbert gravestone, Stirlingshire]

HOWES, WILLIAM, son of Reverend William Howes in Stirling, died in Kingston, Jamaica, on 31 October 1803. [SM.66.79]

HOWIT, THOMAS, a weaver, was admitted as a burgess of Stirling in 1804. [SBR]

HUME, ANDREW, was admitted as a burgess and guilds-brother of Stirling in 1824. [SBR]

HUNTER, ALEXANDER, a coalminer in Coalsnaughton, Tillicoultry, Clackmannanshire, was accused of obstructing, assaulting, officers of the law in 1818. [NRS.AD.14.18.49]

HUNTER, ELIZABETH, a collier of the Square, Clackmannan, was accused of part of a mobbing, rioting, assaulting officers of the law, and rescuing person from lawful custody in Clackmannan in 1842. [NRS.AD14.42.339]

HUNTER, WILLIAM, son of William Hunter a collier in Duke Street, Clackmannan, was accused of part of a mobbing, rioting, assaulting officers of the law, and rescuing person from lawful custody in Clackmannan in 1842. [NRS.AD14.42.339]

HUTCHISON, HENRY, of the Alloa Roperie Company, versus Margaret Whyte or Taylor, in 1827. [NRS.AC8.7374]

HUTCHISON, ROBERT, born 1783 in St Ninian's, Stirling, emigrated to America in 1808, was naturalised in New York on 2 November 1811, a merchant at 143 Pearl Street, New York. [1812] [NYPL.ms]

HUTTON, ANDREW, a writer in Stirling, son of William Hutton a burgess, was admitted as a burgess of Dunfermline, Fife, on 24 October 1809. [DM]

HUTTON, ROBERT, a wright from Blair Drummond, Stirlingshire, son of William Hutton a burgess, was admitted as a burgess of Dunfermline, Fife, on 24 October 1809. [DM]

INGLIS, JAMES, son of Thomas Inglis a feuar in Clackmannan, a Lieutenant of the Maryland Loyalists Regiment, testament, 6 December 1785. [NRS]

INGLIS, JAMES, born in 1778, a farmer at Stockbridge, died on 5 July 1856, husband of Sarah Baird, born in 1782, died on 12 August 1859. [Muiravonside gravestone, Stirlingshire]

INGLIS, WILLIAM, son of Andrew Inglis, a smith at Kennetpans, Clackmannanshire, was apprenticed to Thomas Reid, a clock and watchmaker in Edinburgh, for six years, on 17 October 1799. [ERA]

INGLIS, WILLIAM, was admitted as a burgess and guilds-brother of Stirling in 1838. [SBR]

INGRAM, PETER, born in Clackmannan, an inmate of William Simson's Asylum for 6 months, died there on 21 June 1839. [Muiravonside gravestone, Stirlingshire]

INNES, WILLIAM, born 1770, a minister in Stirling from 1793 until 1794. [F.4.325]

IRVINE, JOHN, was admitted as a burgess and guilds-brother of Stirling in 1825. [SBR]

IZAT, ALEXANDER, owner of the Diligence of Kincardine-on-Forth importing flax from Archangel, Russia, in 1807. [NRS.CS29.5.12.1809]

IZAT, ALEXANDER, a grazier, farmer, and cattle dealer of East Mains of Dollar, Clackmannanshire, sequestration, 1841. [NRS.CS280.27.45.1]

IZAT, ALEXANDER, from Dollar, Clackmannanshire, in the Indian Civil Service, married Maggie D. Rennie, from Falkirk, Stirlingshire, in Bombay, India, on 10 October 1873. [GH.10542]

IZAT, DAVID, a skipper in Alloa, Clackmannanshire, a witness in 1800. [NRS.CC8.8.135]

IZAT, GEORGE, jr., master of the Aid of Kincardine, trading between Alloa and St Petersburg, Russia, in 1816. [NRS.E504.2.13]

IZAT, JOHN, from Alloa, Clackmannanshire, a ship carpenter, later a merchant in Charleston, South Carolina, died on a voyage to Africa in 1800, testament, 1804, Comm. Edinburgh. [NRS] [reference to his brothers, sisters and executors in Scotland – David Izat a skipper in Alloa, Elizabeth Izat, wife of Robert Cusine a wright in Dunfermline, Janet Izat a widow in Clackmannan, Helen Izat a servant in Edinburgh, Thomas Izat a farm servant in Carshill, and Marion Izat. [NRS.CC8.8.135]

IZAT, JOHN, of Upper Mains of Dollar, died on 20 May 1850, husband of Isabel Fergus, who died on 14 September 1836. [Dollar gravestone, Clackmannanshire]

JACK, ALEXANDER, a merchant in Stonywood, Denny, Stirlingshire, father of Anna Jack who married George W. Dickie in San Francisco, California, on 5 August 1873. [GH.10511]

JAFFREY, ALEXANDER, born 1777 in Stirling, a machinist who died in Savannah, Georgia, on 9 April 1810. [Old Colonial gravestone, Savannah]

JAFFRAY, or STRONG, ANN MARIA, born 1818, died at Ewe Burn Station, Otago, New Zealand, on 26 July 1870. [Holy Rude gravestone, Stirling]

JAFFREY, JOHN, a watchmaker in Stirling, a testament, 1793, Comm. Stirling. [NRS]

JAFFREY, JOHN, was admitted as a burgess and guilds-brother of Stirling in 1800. [SBR]

JAFFREY, JOHN, a former baillie of Stirling, settled in Canada in 1820. [NRS.GD51.6.21131]

JAFFRAY, THOMAS, a tanner in St Ninian's, Stirling, later in America, testament, 7 September 1798, Comm. Edinburgh. [NRS]

JAFFREY, Dr WILLIAM, of Cambusbarron in 1828. [SJA.22/5,4D]

JAMESON, JAMES, born 1739, Sheriff Clerk of Clackmannanshire, died 3 December 1823, husband of Margaret Haig, born 1753, died 19 January 1815. [Alloa gravestone, Clackmannanshire]

JAMIESON, ALEXANDER, a baker, was admitted as a burgess of Stirling in 1813. [SBR]

JAMIESON, ALEXANDER, a surgeon in Alloa, Clackmannanshire, in 1826. [SJA.27/7,4A]

JAMIESON, JAMES, master of the <u>Return of Kincardine</u> trading between Alloa and Riga, Latvia, in 1817. [NRS.E504.2.13]

JAMIESON, JAMES, born 1814, a shoemaker, died on 25 September 1871, husband of Margaret McGregor, born 1810, died 8 August 1876. [Alva gravestone, Clackmannanshire]

JAMIESON, THOMAS, a skipper in Tulliallan, Clackmannanshire, testament, 1803, Comm. Dunblane. [NRS]

JARVIE, JAMES, was admitted as a burgess and guilds-brother of Stirling in 1802. [SBR]

JENKINS, JAMES, in Stirling in 1851. [SJA.10/1,4C]

JENKINS, THOMAS, was admitted as a burgess and guilds-brother of Stirling in 1846. [SBR]

JOHNSTON, ALEXANDER, a sailor, son of Thomas Johnston in Falkirk, Stirlingshire, in 1792. [NRS.S/H]

JOHNSTONE, ALLAN, a mechanic, was admitted as a burgess of Stirling in 1807. [SBR]

JOHNSTONE, EBENEZER, editor of the 'Stirling Observer', married Elisabeth Gray, in Bearside, 16 November1837. [SO]

JOHNSTONE, HELEN WALKER, born 14 November 1839, daughter of Reverend Robert John Walker in Auchtermuchty, married Daniel Gibb from San Francisco, California, in Logie, Stirlingshire, on 14 November 1855. [F.4.357] [EEC.788818]

JOHNSTON, JAMES, a weaver in Alva, Stirlingshire, was accused of poaching in 1844. [NRS.AD14.44.390]

JOHNSTON, MARY, of the Balfron Emigration Society, Stirlingshire, from Greenock aboard the <u>David of London</u> bound for Quebec, Canada, on 19 May 1821, was granted land in Lanark, Upper Canada, in 1821. [PAO]

JOHNSTONE or CARRICK, MARY, widow of Charles Carrick a farmer in Baad, Blair Drummond, Stirlingshire, died in December 1850, mother of Robert Carrick in USA. [NRS.S/H]

JOHNSTON, ROBERT, eldest son of James Johnston, a grain merchant in Stirling, died in Batavia, Java, Dutch East Indies, on 2 March 1841. [W.II.165]

JOHNSTON, THOMAS, in Quebec, son and heir of Archibald Johnston, a bookseller in Falkirk, Stirlingshire, who died 18 June 1877. [NRS.S/H]

JOHNSTON, WILLIAM CORBET, a tailor, was admitted as a burgess of Stirling in 1817. [SBR]

JOHNSTONE, Mr, was liberated from Stirling Castle in 1820. [SJA.17/8, 4C]

JONES, GIDEON, master of the Caledonia of Alloa, trading between Shediac, New Brunswick, and Alloa in 1817. [NRS.E504.2.13]

KEILLER, GEORGE THOMSON, born 1847 in Stirling, died in East Moriches, Long Island, New York, on 19 August 1873. [EC.27750] [GH10516]

KEIR, FINLAY, jr., son of Finlay Keir in Daldanit, Aberfoyle, Stirlingshire, a victim of an assault, in 1835. [NRS.AD14.35.107]

KEIR, JOHN, born 1779, son of John Keir a farmer in Stirlingshire, was educated at Glasgow University in 1799, a licentiate of the Secession Church, a minister in Nova Scotia from 1810 to 1827, later Professor of Theology, died on 12 October 1858. [MAGU]

KEIR, PETER, a clock and watchmaker in Falkirk from 1806 until 1830, died 1834. [OSC.108]

KELLY, ANDREW, salesman for McNab Brothers, distillers in Dolls Lodge, Clackmannan, was accused of a breach of trust and embezzlement in 1842. [NRS.AD14.42.467]

KEMP, DAVID, of the Balfron Emigration Society, Stirlingshire, from Greenock aboard the <u>David of London</u> bound for Quebec, Canada, on 19 May 1821, was granted land in Lanark, Upper Canada in December 1821. [PAO]

KENNEDY, DANIEL, born 1815, a physician who died in Grenada on 2 July 1845. [Buchlyvie gravestone, Stirlingshire]

KENT, JOHN, born 1749 in Alloa, Clackmannanshire, son of James Kent, emigrated to Canada, settled in Lower Stewiacke, Nova Scotia. [HT]

KER, ALEXANDER, a piper from Doune, Stirlingshire, was admitted as a burgess and town officer of Dunfermline, Fife, on 10 July 1791. [DM]

KER, ANDREW, son of Robert Ker a farmer in Dennyloanhead, Falkirk, Stirlingshire, was educated at Glasgow University in 1789, a licentiate of the Secession Church in 1798, a minister at Economy, Nova Scotia, before 1816. [MAGU][UPC]

KERR, DAVID, born 5 February 1749 in Menteith, Stirlingshire, emigrated to America in 1769, settled initially in Falmouth, Virginia, and in 1773 in Annapolis, Maryland, died on 2 November 1814. [TSA][BAF]

KERR, DAVID, born 21 May 1839, son of James Kerr, 1820-1860, died at Moonto, Wallaroo, South Australia, in January 1868. [Holy Rude gravestone, Stirling]

KERR, JOHN, a mason in Camelon, Stirlingshire, died 1817. [NRS.S/H]

KERR, WALTER, born 1798, a skipper who was lost at sea in 1827, husband of Margaret Haworth, born 1798, died in March 1860. [Larbert gravestone, Stirlingshire]

KEY, ROBERT, of Rightpark and Edinbelly, born 1744, died 1816, husband of Helen Galbraith, born 1761, died 1832. [Kippen gravestone, Stirlingshire]

KID, GEORGE, a butcher in Alloa, and his wife Mary King, were accused of robbery in 1812. [NRS.AD14.12.99]

KIDSTON, ROBERT, formerly a tenant in Throsk, later in Stirling, testament, 1794, Comm, Stirling. [NRS]

KINCAID, CHARLES, born 1793, son of Joh Kincaid and his wife Margaret Gaff, died in Paarl, Cape of Good Hope, South Africa. [Falkirk gravestone, Stirlingshire]

KINNEMONT, JOHN, master of the Dalmarnock of Alloa trading between Greenock and New York in 1826, also from Alloa to New York in 1828. [NARA.M237]

KIRK, ALEXANDER, born 1782 in Airth, Stirlingshire, a merchant, applied to become a citizen of South Carolina on 2 January 1806. [NARA.M1183.1]

KIRK, ALEXANDER, born 1787 in Grangemouth, Stirlingshire, died in St John, New Brunswick, on 21 July 1834. [New Brunswick Courier, 26.7.1834]

KIRK, SAMUEL, in Kirk's Close, Clackmannan, a victim of rioting etc, there in 1842. [NRS.AD14.42.339]

KIRK, Dr, in Doune, Stirlingshire, in 1841. [SJA.30/7, 4E]

KIRKWOOD, JAMES, born 1742, died 6 April 1819. [Falkirk gravestone, Stirlingshire]

KIRKWOOD, JOHN, born in Stirling, died at Long Point, Montreal, Quebec, on 20 August 1832. [AJ.422]

LAMB, JAMES, in Falkirk, Stirlingshire, a deed, 12 August 1841. [NRS.RD29.3.23]

LAMBIE, JOHN, in Grangemouth, Stirlingshire, in 1855. [SJA.19/10, 3D]

LAMOND, JOHN, found guilty of fraud and fire-raising, was sentenced in Stirling to transportation to the colonies for fourteen years, in 1816. [NRS.GD1.959]

LAMOND, ROBERT, was admitted as a burgess and guilds-brother of Stirling in 1846. [SBR]

LANDERS, ADOLPHUS HAY, son of James Landers in Stirling, died on an expedition into the Shan States, Burma, in 1845. [W.VII.657]

LANDERS, Captain JAMES HENRY, eldest son of James Landers, died on the island of Chusan, China, on 6 October 1840. [W.II.115]

LANG, JAMES, a skipper in Carronshore, Larbert, Stirlingshire, testament, 18 January 1787, Comm. Stirling. [NRS]

LAPSLIE, JAMES, second son of Reverend James Lapslie in Campsie, Stirlingshire, was educated at Glasgow University in 1812, died in Tobago on 23 August 1819. [EA][MAGU] [S.149.19]

LAUDER, CUMBERLAND, an Ensign of the Loyal Stirling Volunteers, was admitted as a burgess and guilds-brother of Dunfermline, Fife, on 17 July 1804. [DM]

LAWRENCE, JOHN, a shipowner in Limekilns, husband of Marion Bullock who died at Alva Manse in November 1822. [Alva gravestone, Clackmannanshire]

LAWSON, THOMAS, master of the Nelly of Kincardine trading between Alloa and Guernsey, in the Channel Islands, in 1815. [NRS.E504.2.13]

LEARMONTH, COLVILLE LIVIGSTON, married George Adam, from Bombay, India, at Parkhall House, Stirling, 29 October 1847. [SO]

LEARMONTH, JOHN, born 1795, died on 28 August 1876, husband of Elizabeth Cochrane, born 1801, died on 20 February 1870. [Muiravonside gravestone, Stirlingshire]

LEARMONTH, PETER, son of Hugh Learmonth, [1795-1870], and his wife Janet Boag, [1811-1881], settled in Australia. [Polmont gravestone, Stirlingshire]

LEARMONTH, THOMAS, son of Hugh Learmonth, [1795-1870], and his wife Janet Boag, [1811-1881], settled in Australia. [Polmont gravestone, Stirlingshire]

LECKIE, JAMES, son of William Leckie of Brioch, Stirlingshire, died in St James, Jamaica, on 24 August 1792. [SM.54.570]

LECKIE, JOHN, born 1835, son of William Leckie and his wife Eleanor McFarlan, died in Manitoba in 1895. [Kippen gravestone, Stirlingshire]

LEECH, MATTHEW, a former Captain of the Stirlingshire Militia, applied to settle in Canada on 8 March 1819. [TNA.CO384.5.77]; settled in Brockville, Upper Canada, before 1823. [NLS.ms10959/154,256]

LEGGATE, ARCHIBALD, a Lieutenant of the Clackmannan Volunteers, was admitted as a burgess and guilds-brother of Dunfermline, Fife, on 24 February 1804. [DM]

LEISHMAN, JOHN, master of the snow Nancy, son of Abraham Leishman, a merchant in Falkirk, Stirlingshire, in 1797. [NRS.S/H]

LEISHMAN, WILLIAM, born 1 May 1785 in Falkirk, Stirlingshire, a merchant in Halifax, Nova Scotia, died in Edinburgh on 31 October 1871. [New Calton gravestone, Edinburgh]

LENNIE, GEORGE, born 1768, died 4 December 1842, husband of Margaret Gilfillan, born 1754, died 14 May 1813. [Balfron gravestone, Stirlingshire]

LENNOX, COLLIN, a slater in Doune, Stirlingshire, was admitted as a burgess of Dunfermline, Fife, on 4 August 1791. [DM]

LENNY, JANET, from Balfron, Stirlingshire, settled in America by 1819. [NRS.CS17.1.39/23]

LIDDELL, JOHN, from Dennyloanhead, Stirlingshire, a minister in Amherst, Nova Scotia, from 1817 until 1817, died in Bonnybridge, Stirlingshire, on 20 June 1844. [UPC]

LIDDELL, JOHN, master of the Caledonia of Alloa, with passengers bound from Leith to Australia on 17 April 1839, landed at Port Philip, Victoria, Australia, on 18 September 1839. [Leith Commercial Lists, 27.2728/2742/2809]

LIGHTBODY, JAMES, son of George Lightbody and his wife Janet Lyle, died on 17 April 1887 and was buried at Beechwood, Victoria, Australia. [Falkirk gravestone, Stirlingshire]

LINDSAY, DAVID, born 1757, minister at Clackmannan for 45 years, died on 21 October 1834, husband of Margaret Jeffery who was born in July 1777. [Clackmannan gravestone]

LINKLETTER, ROBERT, a weaver, son of Robert Linkletter, was admitted as a burgess of Stirling in 1854. [SBR]

LIVINGSTONE, WILLIAM, MD, born 1803, from Kilsyth, Stirlingshire, died in St John, New Brunswick, on 1 January 1875. [EC.28174]

LIVINGSTONE, WILLIAM, of the Deanston Emigration Society, Stirlingshire, with his wife and son, from Greenock aboard the David of London bound for Quebec, Canada, on 19 May 1821, was granted land in Lanark, Upper Canada by 9 September 1821, and in 24 March 1822. [PAO]

LOCKHART, JAMES, son of William Lockhart, was admitted as a burgess and guilds-brother of Stirling in 1850. [SBR]

LOCKHART, JAMES GALBRAITH, born 1840, son of John Lockhart and his wife Frances Downie Galbraith, died in Dunedin, New Zealand, on 26 October 1863. [Stirling, Holy Rude gravestone]

LOGAN, JESSIE, of Dunmore Park, died in New South Wales, Australia, 23 December 1841. [SO]

LOGAN, JOHN, born 1811 in Lettermill, Killearn, Stirlingshire, died in Farmington, Warren County, Pennsylvania, on 8 March 1879. [EC.29491]

LOGAN, ROBERT, a skipper in Grangemouth, Stirlingshire, testament, 1813. [NRS]

LOGAN, WILLIAM, was admitted as a burgess and guilds-brother of Stirling in 1849. [SBR]

LONDON, JAMES, of the Alloa Emigration Society, from Greenock aboard the David of London bound for Quebec, Canada, on 19 May 1821, was granted land in Lanark, Upper Canada in 1821. [PAO]

LOVE, ANDREW, master of the St Lawrence of Grangemouth from Greenock bound for Newfoundland in 1816 also in 1817. [NRS.E504.15.111/115]

LOW, JAMES, son of James Low, [1794-1859], and his wife Elizabeth Young, [died 1831], settled in Salt Lake City, Utah, by 1881. [Holy Rude gravestone, Stirling]

LOWNDES, JOHN, born 1780 in Stirling, a mariner who was naturalised in South Carolina on 16 October 1805. [NARA.M1183.1]

LUCAS, JAMES, a writer in Stirling in 1840. [SJA.5/6, 4D]

LUCAS, WALTER, was admitted as a burgess and guilds-brother of Stirling in 1834. [SBR]

LUNN, AGNES, born 1790 in Campsie, Stirlingshire, died in South Africa on 18 October 1878. [St George gravestone, Port Elizabeth]

LYALL, J. W., the reporter of Falkirk, Stirlingshire, in 1852. [SJA.10/12,4C]

LYELL, DAVID, in Clackmannan in 1848. [SJA.31/3,4C]

LYELL, JOHN, in Bridge of Allan, Stirlingshire, father of John Lyell, born 1865, who died in an accident in San Saba, Texas, on 30 November 1897. [S.17017]

LYLE, JAMES, a merchant in Virginia, later in Meadowhead of Strathblane, Stirlingshire, testament, Comm. Glasgow. [NRS]

LYON, DAVID, son of Walter Lyon, was admitted as a burgess and guilds-brother of Stirling in 1843. [SBR]

MACADAM, JAMES, born 1769 in Drymen, Stirlingshire, a merchant who was naturalised in South Carolina on 17 June 1799. [NARA.M1183.1]

MCALLASTER, JOHN, a weaver, was admitted as a burgess of Stirling in 1804. [SBR]

MCALLUM, ROBERT, in Stirling in 1852. [SJA.19/11.4B]

MCALLEY, WILLIAM, a mechanic, was admitted as a burgess and guilds-brother of Stirling in 1819. [SBR]

MCALPINE, ROBERT, [1814-1863], and his wife Janet Currie, [1818-1891], parents of Daniel Currie McAlpine, born 1857, died in Hoytdale, Pennsylvania, on 15 March 1903. [St Ninian's gravestone, Stirling]

MCALPINE, WILLIAM, in Buchlyvie, Stirlingshire, in 1858. [SJA.2/8,5D]

MCARA, C., agent of the Union Bank of Scotland in Dunblane, Stirlingshire, in 1849. [POD]

MCARA, Mr, an innkeeper in Stirling in 1844. [SJA.2/8, 4C]

MCAREE, WILLIAM, jr., a mechanic, was admitted as a burgess of Stirling in 1824. [SBR]

MCARTHUR, DUNCAN, son of Duncan McArthur, [1756-1844], a farmer in Gurleston, and his wife Margaret Sands, [1757-1842], a mason who died in the West Indies aged 31. [Port of Menteith gravestone, Stirlingshire]

MCARTHUR, ROBERT, in Stirling Post Office in 1848. [SJA.10/3,4E]

MCARTHUR, ROBERT, in Tucksmith, Rodgerville, Canada West, grandson and heir of Robert McArthur, a dyer in Callendar, Stirlingshire, who died on 13 September 1832. [NRS.S/H]

MCBEATH, or WRIGHT, HELEN, a gardener in Stirling, heir to her son James McBeath in New York, in 1834. [NRS.S/H]

MCBEATH, JOHN, was admitted as a burgess of Stirling in 1816. [SBR]

MCCALLUM, JAMES, a clock and watchmaker in Falkirk around 1800. [OSC.108]

MCCALLUM, DUNCAN, born 1794, a labourer in Aberfoyle, Stirlingshire, emigrated via Port Glasgow on the Favourite of St John bound for St John, New Brunswick, on 22 October 1815. [PANB.ms.RS23E.9798]

MCCOWANE, PETER, was admitted as a burgess and guilds-brother of Stirling in 1804. [SBR]

MACCRAIRE, or HENDERSON, ROBINA, in Falkirk, Stirlingshire, dead by 1819. [NRS.S/H]

MCCRONE, JAMES, was admitted as a burgess and guilds-brother of Stirling in 1832. [SBR]

MCCULLOCH, PETER, sub agent of the Edinburgh and Glasgow Bank in Alva, Clackmannanshire, in 1849. [POD]

MCDIARMID, DANIEL, was admitted as a burgess of Stirling in 1810. [SBR]

MCDIARMID, JOHN, a post runner in Kippen, Stirlingshire, in 1862. [SJA.29/8,4F]

MCDONALD, GEORGE, born 1790, a labourer in Falkirk, Stirlingshire, emigrated via Port Glasgow aboard the Favourite of St John, master John Hyndman, bound for St John, New Brunswick, on 22 October 1815. [PANB.ms.RS23E.9798]

MCDONALD, JOHN, was admitted as a burgess and guilds-brother of Stirling in 1804. [SBR]

MCDONALD, JOHN, from Stirling, clerk of the Commissary's office in Sydney, New South Wales, Australia, in 1835. [NRS.GD171/1219.47-48]

MCDONALD, SAMUEL, a merchant, died in Spittal, Square, Stirling, 17 November 1853. [SO]

MCDOUGALL, A., master of the Monarch of Alloa from Greenock to Miramachi, New Brunswick, on 9 August 1819, and between Leith and Miramachi, New Brunswick, in 1820. [NRS.E504.15.125; E504.22.91]

MCDOUGAL, JAMES, master of the Alert of Alloa trading between Riga, Latvia, and Alloa in 1815. [NRS.E504.2.13]

MCDOUGALL, PETER, in California, nephew and heir to Christian Duff or McLeary in Bridge of Allan, Stirlingshire, who died on 18 May 1877. [NRS.S/H]

MCDOUGAL, Mr, the criminal officer of Campsie, Stirlingshire, in 1838. [SJA.30/3,4E]

MCEWAN, DANIEL KENNEDY, MD, born 1815, son of John McEwan and his wife Helen Louttet, died in Grenada, on 2 July 1845. [Buchlyvie gravestone, Stirlingshire]

MCEWAN, GEORGE, '38 years in medical practice in Grenada', died in Edinburgh on 17 October 1834. [Port of Menteith gravestone, Stirlingshire]

MCEWAN, JAMES, master of the Nelly of Alloa trading between Alloa and Dublin, Ireland, in 1816. [NRS.E504.2.13]

MCEWAN, JOHN, a shipowner, died on 13 January 1832, husband of Ann Jeffrey, born 1802, died 7 October 1879. [Alloa gravestone, Clackmannanshire]

MCEWAN, MARY, eldest daughter of James McEwan, of South Lodge, Stirling, married Louis Wilhelm Bode, a Lieutenant of the Royal Hanoverian Leib Regiment, at the British Consulate in Cologne, and later at the English chapel of the Prince of Prussia in Koblenz on 4 January 1858. [W.XIX.1980]

MCEWAN, JOHN, of the Crieff Banking Company in 1853. [SJA.10/6.3D]

MCFARLANE, ALEXANDER, born 1790, a labourer in Callander, Stirlingshire, emigrated via Port Glasgow aboard the Favourite of St John, master John Hyndman, bound for St John, New Brunswick, on 22 October 1815. [PANB.ms.RS23E.9798]

MACFARLANE, ALEXANDER, agent of the Bank of Scotland in Falkirk, Stirlingshire, in 1849. [POD]

MACFARLANE, ALEXANDER, the younger of Thornhill, born 19 October 1828, died on 1 December 1871, father of Alexander MacFarlane, born 29 December 1852, died in Wellington, New

Zealand, on 3 October 1880, and John Scott MacFarlane, born 3 October 1856, who died at Humansdorp, South Africa, on 21 September 1883. [Alloa gravestone, Clackmannanshire]

MCFARLANE, ANDREW, born 1790 in Milngavie, Stirlingshire, a merchant in New York by 1826, died at the Belmont Hotel on 3 January 1873. [ANY]

MACFARLANE, DUNCAN, born 1810 in the Port of Menteith, Stirlingshire, died at the Karn Melks River, Caledon, South Africa, on 25 July 1884. [S.12838]

MCFARLANE, Reverend HUGH, born 1780, son of John McFarlane, a farmer in St Ninian's, Stirlingshire, graduated MA, MD from Glasgow University, minister of St Andrew's Presbyterian Church in Nassau, New Providence in the Bahamas until his death there on 20 September 1817. [F.7.666][S.1.46] [MAGU]

MCFARLANE, HUGH, and MALCOLM, GRAHAM, both in Gartmore, Stirlingshire, were victims of forgery, 1851. [NRS.AD14.51.522]

MCFARLANE, JAMES, of Woodside Cottage, Doune, Stirlingshire, an architect, builder and parish elder, Master of the Lodge St James number 171 from 1808 until 1809, 1811. [DHN.iii]

MCFARLANE, JANET, born 13 September 1793, daughter of Donald McFarlane and his wife Mary McNee in Stirlingshire, emigrated to North America in 1821, settled in Huntingdon, Quebec, died there on 25 November 1869. [CMF]

MCFARLANE, MALCOLM, in Gartmore, Stirlingshire, a victim of forgery, 1851. [NRS.AD14.51.522]

MCFARLANE, PARLAN, born 25 May 1795, son of Donald McFarlane and his wife Mary McNee in Stirlingshire, emigrated to North America in 1819, settled in Huntingdon, Quebec, died on 12 June 1860. [CMF]

MCFARLANE, PETER, born 25 February 1797, son of Donald McFarlane and his wife Mary McNee in Stirlingshire, emigrated to North America in 1819, settled in Huntingdon, Quebec, died on 9 October 1870. [CMF]

MACFARLANE, THOMAS, born 1789 in Alloa, Clackmannanshire, died in St Andrews, New Brunswick, on 25 August 1840. [New Brunswick Courier, 5.9.1840]

MCFARLANE, WILLIAM, a baker in Stirling in 1825. [SJA.3/11.1C]

MCFARLANE, Mr, an innkeeper in Stirling in 1848. [SJA.7/7,4E]

MACFIE, JOHN, a weaver, was admitted as a burgess of Stirling in 1824. [SBR]

MCGIBBON, JAMES, was admitted as a burgess and guilds-brother of Stirling in 1826. [SBR]

MCGIBBON, JOHN, overseer of Bargunnock House, married Isabella Monteith, at Blair Drummond, Stirlingshire, 29 January 1846. [SO]

MCGILCHRIST, JAMES, born 1711, died 2 December 1794. [Falkirk gravestone, Stirlingshire]

MCGILCHRIST, JAMES, a farmer of Ballat, Balfron, Stirlingshire, married Mary McGilchrist, in Fintry, Stirlingshire, 2 July 1844. [SO]

MCGILL, JOHN, was admitted as a burgess and guilds-brother of Stirling in 1804. [SBR]

MCGOWAN, WILLIAM, of the Alloa Industrial School, Stirlingshire, in 1856. [SJA.19/12,2G]

MCGOWAN, WILLIAM, born 1807, a physician in Alloa, died 22 December 1858, husband of [1] Margaret Moubray, born 1811, died 11 December 1845, [2] Elizabeth Bald, born 1804, died 8 October 1868. [Alloa gravestone, Clackmannanshire]

MCGREGOR, ALEXANDER, born 1797 in Denny, Stirlingshire, a merchant in Charleston, South Carolina, was admitted as a citizen on 29 September 1827. [NARA.M1183.1]

MCGREGOR, ALEXANDER, born 1799, died 20 September 1884, husband of Catherine Whyte, who died on 12 February 1879. [Alloa gravestone, Clackmannanshire]

MCGREGOR, DONALD, born 1777, from Doune, Stirlingshire, with his wife Agnes born 1788, and children William born 1801, Mary born 1803, Elizabeth born 1807, Grizel born 1810, and Jane born 1812, emigrated via Port Glasgow aboard the Favourite of St John, master John Hyndman, bound for St John, New Brunswick, on 22 October 1815. [PANB.ms.RS23E.9798]

MCGREGOR, DONALD, born 1781, a labourer in Callendar, Stirlingshire, emigrated via Port Glasgow aboard the Favourite of St John, master John Hyndman, bound for St John, New Brunswick, on 22 October 1815. [PANB.ms.RS23E.9798]

MCGREGOR, DONALD, born 1781, a labourer in Callendar, Stirlingshire, emigrated via Port Glasgow aboard the Favourite of St John, master John Hyndman, bound for St John, New Brunswick, on 22 October 1815. [PANB.ms.RS23E.9798]

MCGREGOR, DUNCAN, born 1775, a labourer in Callendar, Stirlingshire, with his wife Janet born 1776, and children Catherine born 1795, Margaret born 1797, Gregor born 1798, Isabella born 1800, Mary born 1801, Marjorie born 1803, James born 1809, and Elizabeth born 1809, emigrated via Port Glasgow aboard the Favourite of St John, master John Hyndman, bound for St John, New Brunswick, on 22 October 1815. [PANB.ms.RS23E.9798]

MCGREGOR, ISABELLA, born 1 November 1830 in Crieff, Perthshire, daughter of James McGregor, [1787-1837], and his wife Margaret Ferguson, [1793-1842], died in Cleveland, Ohio, on 4 January 1891. [Tillicoultry gravestone, Clackmannanshire]

MCGREGOR, JAMES, born 1800, a labourer in Callendar, Stirlingshire, emigrated via Port Glasgow aboard the Favourite of St John, master John Hyndman, bound for St John, New Brunswick, on 22 October 1815. [PANB.ms.RS23E.9798]

MCGREGOR, JOHN, born 1794, a labourer in Callendar, Stirlingshire, emigrated via Port Glasgow aboard the Favourite of St John, master John Hyndman, bound for St John, New Brunswick, on 22 October 1815. [PANB.ms.RS23E.9798]

MCGREGOR, KATHERINE, born 1 June 1826 in Crieff, Perthshire, daughter of James McGregor, [1787-1837], and his wife Margaret Ferguson, [1793-1842], died in Newark, New Jersey, on 5 December 1893. [Tillicoultry gravestone, Clackmannanshire]

MCGREGOR, MARGARET, born 15 September 1827 in Crieff, Perthshire, daughter of James McGregor, [1787-1837], and his wife Margaret Ferguson, [1793-1842], died in Cleveland, Ohio, on 31 August 1859, wife of Richard Huddlestone. [Tillicoultry gravestone, Clackmannanshire]

MCGREGOR, PETER, born 1781, a labourer in Callendar, Stirlingshire, emigrated via Port Glasgow aboard the Favourite of St John, master John Hyndman, bound for St John, New Brunswick, on 22 October 1815. [PANB.ms.RS23E.9798]

MCGREGOR, PETER, born 1813 a labourer in Callendar, Stirlingshire, emigrated via Port Glasgow aboard the Favourite of St John, master John Hyndman, bound for St John, New Brunswick, on 22 October 1815. [PANB.ms.RS23E.9798]

MCGREGOR, WILLIAM, a weaver in Alva, Stirlingshire, was accused of poaching in 1844. [NRS.AD14.44.390]

MCGREGOR, Mr, from Callander, Stirlingshire, emigrated in 1858. [SJA.31/12,4F]

MCGRIGGOR, JAMES, a clock and watchmaker in Balfron, Stirlingshire around 1825. [OSC.108]

MCILWRAITH, JOHN, born 1846 in Stirling, died in Port Elizabeth, South Africa, in 1918. [St George gravestone, Port Elizabeth]

MCINDOE, JAMES, in Carbeth, Strathblane, Stirlingshire, dead by 1822, uncle of Walter McIndoe a merchant in Petersburg, Virginia. [NRS.S/H]

MCINNES, THOMAS G., born 1791, son of Neil McInnes a manufacturer in Logie, Stirlingshire, was educated at Glasgow University in 1808, a minister in Halifax, Nova Scotia, from 1815 until

1820, later a minister in Philadelphia, Pennsylvania, from 1820 until his death on 26 August 1824. [MAGU]

MCINTOSH, DANIEL, was admitted as a burgess and guilds-brother of Stirling in 1801. [SBR]

MCINTOSH, THOMAS, a farmer in St Vincent, Canada West, grandson and heir of John Kinross, a vintner in Dunblane, Stirlingshire, who died on 31 May 1827. [NRS.S/H]

MCINTOSH, Dr, from Denny, Stirlingshire, now in Canada in 1855. [SJA.20/4,3E]

MCINTOSH, Mr, of the chemical works at Grangemouth, Stirlingshire, in 1845. [SJA.6/6,4D]

MCINTYRE, JAMES, died 15 November 1870, husband of Margaret Morrison, died 20 July 1852. [Alloa gravestone, Clackmannanshire]

MCINTYRE, MALCOLM, born 1779, a labourer in Callendar, Stirlingshire, emigrated via Port Glasgow aboard the Favourite of St John, master John Hyndman, bound for St John, New Brunswick, on 22 October 1815. [PANB.ms.RS23E.9798]

MCINTYRE, MARGARET, c/o Mrs Ross in Friars Wynd, Stirling, was accused of theft in 1837. [NRS.AD14.37.207]

MCINTYRE, PETER, born 1782, a labourer in Callendar, Stirlingshire, with his wife Jean born 1782, and children – Jean born 1809, John born 1811, and Janet born 1813, emigrated via Port Glasgow aboard the Favourite of St John, master John Hyndman, bound for St John, New Brunswick, on 22 October 1815. [PANB.ms.RS23E.9798]

MACKAY, JOHN S., agent of the Commercial Bank of Scotland in Grangemouth, Stirlingshire, in 1849. [POD]

MACKAY, JAMES, a farmer in Wester Ballat, Stirlingshire, heir to his great grandfather Charles McKay, a planter in Jamaica, in 1860. [NRS.SH]

MACKAY, JAMES DRUMMOND, in Toronto, Ontario, heir to his grandmother Elizabeth Gibb, wife of James Drummond a merchant in Stirling, who died on 9 June 1879, re property in Bothwell, Lanarkshire. [NRS.S/H]

MCKAY, MUNGO CAMPBELL, a merchant from Stirling, was naturalised in South Carolina on 31 May 1798. [NARA.M1183.1]

MCKENDRICK, JAMES, a weaver, was admitted as a burgess and of Stirling in 1802. [SBR]

MCKENDRICK, JOHN, was admitted as a burgess and guilds-brother of Stirling in 1814. [SBR]

MCKENZIE, JOHN, master of the Dunlop of Grangemouth, Stirlingshire, trading between Greenock and Quebec in 1811. [NRS.E504.15.93]

MCKENZIE, ROBERT, Ensign of the Loyal Stirling Volunteers, was admitted as a burgess and guilds-brother of Dunfermline, Fife, on 17 July 1804. [DM]

MCKENZIE, WILLIAM, a weaver in Alva, Stirlingshire, was accused of poaching in 1844. [NRS.AD14.44.390]

MCKERRACHER, GEORGE, born 1792, in Gartur, died 25 May 1851, his sister Mary McKerracher, born 1800, died 17 June 1857. [Balfron gravestone, Stirlingshire]

MCKILLOP, ROBERT, a weaver, was admitted as a burgess of Stirling in 1802. [SBR]

MCKINLAY, DONALD, born 1779, a labourer in Callander, Stirlingshire, with his wife Margaret born 1782, and children Margaret born 1811 and John born 1813, emigrated via Port Glasgow aboard the Favourite of St John, master John Hyndman, bound for St John, New Brunswick, on 22 October 1815. [PANB.ms.RS23E.9798]

MCKINLAY, JOHN, born in Stirling, was educated at Glasgow University, emigrated to Nova Scotia in 1817, a missionary and teacher in Pictou, N.S., from 1824 until his death on 20 October 850. [History of the Presbyterian Church, Toronto, 1885]

MCKINLAY, JOHN, son of John McKinlay a farmer in Falkirk, Stirlingshire, was educated at Glasgow University from 1804 until 1813, a minister in Pictou, Nova Scotia. [MAGU]

MCLACHLAN, GEORGE, born 1781, in Hosh, died 26 April 1855, Lachlan McLachlan, born 1799, a teacher in Auchentroig, died 10 September 1846, Margaret McLachlan, born 1785, died 20 October 1872, Mary Lachlan, born 1797, died 2 July 1875. [Balfron gravestone, Stirlingshire]

MCLACHLAN, JAMES, a farmer in Sauchiemill, Stirlingshire, later in Torbrex, dead by 1848, brother of William McLachlan a farmer in Nova Scotia. [NRS.S/H]

MCLAGAN, WILLIAM, from Falkirk, Stirlingshire, later in Leyhead, Tullich, Aberdeenshire, testament, 1794, Comm. Aberdeen. [NRS]

MCLAREN, ARCHIBALD, born 1796, in Callander, Stirlingshire, emigrated via Port Glasgow aboard the Favourite of St John, master John Hyndman, bound for St John, New Brunswick, on 22 October 1815. [PANB.ms.RS23E.9798]

MCLAREN, ARCHIBALD, and his wife Isabella, in Callander, Stirlingshire, a victim of crime in 1831. [NRS.AD14.31.4]

MCLAREN, CATHERINE, daughter of Duncan McLaren in Stirling, married Archibald Kerr a merchant, in Hamilton, Upper Canada, on 6 March 1839. [SG.8.767]

MCLAREN, CATHERINE, wife of R. Smith in Canada, heir to her grandmother Catherine Paton or Fulton in Dollar, Clackmannanshire, in 1854. [NRS.SH]

MCLAREN, ELLEN, in Smith Falls, Lanark, Ontario, cousin and heir of Donald McLaren, a merchant in Callander, Stirlingshire, who died on 7 February 1880. [NRS.S/H]

MCLAREN, JAMES, in Callander, Stirlingshire, a victim of a crime in 1831. [NRS.AD14.31.4]

MCLAREN, JANE, born 1819 in Callander, Stirlingshire, was accused of theft at Duchray Castle, Drymen, Stirling, in 1848. [NRS.AD14.48.403]

MCLAREN, JANET, born 1791, from Callander, Stirlingshire, emigrated via Port Glasgow aboard the Favourite of St John, master John Hyndman, bound for St John, New Brunswick, on 22 October 1815. [PANB.ms.RS23E.9798]

MCLAREN, JOHN, master of the Maria of Kincardine trading between Alloa and Waterford, Ireland, in 1816; master of the Bee of Kincardine trading between Alloa and Riga, Latvia, in 1817. [NRS.E504.2.13]

MCLAREN, MARGARET, wife of Robert Walker, died in Grahamston, Falkirk, Stirlingshire, 13 November 1845. [SO]

MCLAREN, or MCGREGOR, MARGARET ANN, in Smith Falls, Lanark, Ontario, cousin and heir of Donald McLaren, a merchant in Callander, Stirlingshire, who died on 7 February 1880. [NRS.S/H]

MCLAREN, or JOHNSTON, MARY, in Smith Falls, Lanark, Ontario, cousin and heir of Donald McLaren, a merchant in Callander, Stirlingshire, who died on 7 February 1880. [NRS.S/H]

MCLAREN, PETER, born 10 August 1778, farmer at Diverswell, died on 4 October 1867, husband of Janet Allan, born 31 December 1781, died on 1 February 1865. [Clackmannan gravestone]

MCLAREN, ROBERT, born 1778, a labourer in Callander, Stirlingshire, emigrated via Port Glasgow aboard the Favourite of St John, master John Hyndman, bound for St John, New Brunswick, on 22 October 1815. [PANB.ms.RS23E.9798]

MCLAUCHLAN, DOUGAL, of Balwill, later in Stirling, a testament, 1792, Comm. Stirling. [NRS]

MCLAUCHLAN, JAMES, born 1816, son of William McLauchlan and his wife Sarah McFarlane, died in Cleveland, Ohio, on 12 November 1870. [Buchlyvie gravestone, Stirlingshire]

MCLAUCHLAN, ROBERT, born 1826, son of William McLauchlan and his wife Sarah McFarlane, died in Cleveland, Ohio, in 1904. [Buchlyvie gravestone, Stirlingshire]

MCLAUCHLAN, WILLIAM, born 1793, died in Galt, Ontario, on 11 March 1882. [Buchlyvie gravestone, Stirlingshire]

MCLAUGHLAN, WILLIAM, born 1793, married [1] Sarah McFarlane, [1788-1837], [2] Margaret Neilson, [1800-1882]; died in Galt, Upper Canada, on 11 March 1882. [Buchlyvie gravestone, Stirlingshire]

MCLAY, JANE, born 1796, wife of Robert McLew of Cammoquhill, died 14 February 1822. [Balfron gravestone, Stirlingshire]

MCLEA, ARCHIBALD, messenger at arms, Stirling, 1849. [POD]

MCLEAN, CHARLES, an Excise officer in Killin, Stirlingshire, was accused of assault in 1831. [NRS.AD14.31.47]

MCLEAN, THOMAS ANNAN, in Moncton, New Brunswick, son and heir of Mary Alexander or McLean, in Cambus, Alloa, Clackmannanshire, who died on 29 August 1878. [NRS.S/H]

MCLENNAN, MURDOCH, born 1800 in Stirlingshire, died in South Carolina on 4 November 1823. [Prince George Winyah, Georgetown, S.C., gravestone]

MCLUCKIE, JAMES, a mechanic, was admitted as a burgess of Stirling in 1816. [SBR]

MACMEMINY, ROBERT, in Christie's Land, Drygate Street, Stirling, the victim of fraud in 1823. [NRS.AD14.23.126]

MCMICKING, THOMAS, agent of the Union Bank of Scotland in Stirling in 1849. [POD]

MCMILLAN, JOHN, born 14 March 1793 in Camelon, Falkirk, Stirlingshire, son of Duncan McMillan and his wife Mary Bird, a blacksmith in Camelon, fought at Bonnymuir during the Uprising of 1820, found guilty at Stirling of rebellion, was transported to New South Wales, Australia, in 1821, was granted a Certificate of Freedom in 1827, he settled in Sydney in Government service, his wife Jane Gardner and their daughters joined him in 1832, he ran the Blacksmith's Arms pub in Windmill Street, Darling Harbour, Sydney, NSW, from 1836 to 1838, and died at Comely Park, Lane Cove, in 1870. [TSR] [Sydney Morning Herald, 29.8.1877][NRS.NRAS.0347]

MACNAB, JAMES, born 1817, son of John MacNab, [1757-1837], at his wife Christine Buchanan, [1786-1845], died in Arthur township, Canada, on 29 March 1872. [Buchanan gravestone, Stirlingshire]

MCNAB, JOHN, a mason in Callander, Stirlingshire, was accused of assault in 1831. [NRS.AD14.31.47]

MCNAIR, JAMES, second son of Reverend James McNair in Slamannan, Stirlingshire, died in Mobile, Alabama, on 3 October 1823. [F.1.229][BM.15.131]

MCNAIR, WILLIAM, a weaver, was admitted as a burgess of Stirling in 1804. [SBR]

MCNAUGHTON, PETER, an Excise officer at Bridge of Allan, Stirlingshire, married Elizabeth Baird, there, 29 May 1845. [SO]

MCNAUGHTON, ROBERT, was admitted as a burgess and guildsbrother of Stirling in 1820. [SBR]

MCNEIL, NEIL, born 1781 in Buchanan, Stirlingshire, a grocer in Charleston, South Carolina, was naturalised there on 14 October 1806, died 28 March 1851, buried in St Michael's, Charleston. [NARA.M1183.1][St Michael's gravestone]

MCNEILL, ..., son of Walter McNeill sr., a labourer in Gartmore, Stirlingshire, was accused of assault in 1835. [NRS.AD14.35.107]

MCNEILL, ROBERT, a carrier in Gartmore, Stirlingshire, was accused of assault in 1835. [NRS.AD14.35.107]

MCNEILL, WALTER, jr., a carter in Gartmore, Stirlingshire, was accused of assault in 1835. [NRS.AD14.35.107]

MCNEISH, JOHN, born 1785 in Largo, Fife, a merchant in Falkirk, Stirlingshire, with his wife Janet, and five children, emigrated to USA, and was naturalised in New York on 5 February 1828. [NARA]

MCNEISH, JOHN, a clock and watchmaker in Falkirk around 1805. [OSC.108]

MCNICHOLL, ALEXANDER, of the Deanston Emigration Society, Stirlingshire, with his wife, from Greenock aboard the David of London bound for Quebec, Canada, on 19 May 1821, was granted land in Lanark, Upper Canada by 6 August 1821. [PAO]

MCNICOL, DANIEL, born 1813, died 3 July 1873, father of Daniel McNicol who died in Richmond, Virginia, on 14 June 1888. [Campsie gravestone, Stirlingshire]

MCNICOL, PETER, was admitted as a burgess and guilds-brother of Stirling in 1835. [SBR]

MCNIE, DAVID, was accused of assault and robbery in Cow Wynd, Falkirk, Stirlingshire, in 1824. [NRS.AD14.24.234]

MCNIE, WILLIAM, was admitted as a burgess of Stirling in 1821. [SBR]

MCNIVEN, DUNCAN, born 1840, son of John McNiven, a farmer at Westerton, died 15 September 1897, husband of Mary Mackison, born 1844, died at Oldhall on 5 August 1912. [Kippen gravestone, Stirlingshire]

MCNIVEN, JOHN, born 1802, a farmer at Glen Terran, died 29 November 1866, husband of Margaret.... [Kippen gravestone, Stirlingshire]

MCNURE, JAMES, was admitted as a burgess and guilds-brother of Stirling in 1804. [SBR]

MCOSTRICK, ROBERT, a cordiner, was admitted as a burgess of Stirling in 1804. [SBR]

MCOWAT, Captain, of the Thames of Alloa from Alloa, Clackmannanshire, to St John, New Brunswick, in 1856. [LCL]

MACPHERSON, FINLAY, born 11 March 1821, minister of the Free Church in Larbert, died on 7 December 1893. [Larbert East gravestone, Stirlingshire]

MCPHIE, JOHN, with his wife, his son, and six daughters, of the Balfron Emigration Society, Stirlingshire, from Greenock aboard the

David of London bound for Quebec, Canada, on 19 May 1821, was granted land in Lanark, Upper Canada on 6 September 1821. [PAO]

MCQUAT, JAMES, born 1800, died 2 March 1829. [Balfron gravestone, Stirlingshire]

MCQUEEN, GEORGE, a maltman, was admitted as a burgess of Stirling in 1811. [SBR]

MCQUEEN, THOMAS, and his wife Jean Thomson, 1823. [Falkirk gravestone, Stirlingshire]

MCROBIE, DANIEL, of Airthrey Mills, Stirlingshire, married Helen Robertson, in Stirling, 18 January 1844. [SO]

MCRUAR, JOHN, a mason in School Lane and a kirk elder in Doune, Stirlingshire, Master of the Lodge St James number 171 from 1824 - 1825. [DHN.iii]

MCVEY, ROBERT, born 1813, died on 23 February 1890, husband of Isabella Simpson, born 1815, died on 26 June 1851. [Larbert gravestone, Stirlingshire]

MCVEY, WILLIAM, a skipper in Craigtown, Clackmannan, testament, 24 April 1792, Comm. Stirling. [NRS]

MCVICAR, J. ROSS, a banker at Bridge of Allan, Stirlingshire, in 1841. [SJA.10/9.4D]

MCWALTER, MOSES, a clock and watchmaker in Balfron, Stirlingshire, around 1836. [OSC.108]

MCWATT, DAVID, a clerk in Alloa, Clackmannanshire, in 1859. [SJA.s12/8, 6f]

MAIBEN, JOHN, son of Henry Maiben, was admitted as a burgess and guilds-brother of Stirling in 1829. [SBR]

MAILER, JOHN, born 1796, a builder, died 23 December 1857, husband of Elizabeth Blair, born 1802, died 3 September 1870. [Alloa gravestone, Clackmannanshire]

MAIN, THOMAS, born 1763, died at Stirling on 31 July 1835, husband of Jane Rennie, born 1767, died in Stirling on 17 February 1851. [Alloa gravestone, Clackmannanshire]

MALCOLM, FRANCIS, a weaver, was admitted as a burgess of Stirling in 1845. [SBR]

MALCOLM, HENRY, in Dunblane, Stirlingshire, in 1851. [SJA.5/12,4C]

MALCOLM, JAMES, a weaver in Tillicoultry, Clackmannanshire, was accused of theft in 1840. [NRS.AD14.40.416]

MALCOLM, JAMES, a coalminer in Coalsnaughton, Tillicoultry, Clackmannanshire, was accused of obstructing, assaulting, officers of the law in 1818. [NRS.AD.14.18.49]

MALLOCH, ANDREW, was admitted as a burgess of Stirling in 1804. [SBR]

MALLOCH, JAMES CHRYSTAL, in Chisham Square, New York, son and heir of Andrew Malloch, a writer in Dunblane, Stirlingshire, who died on 4 February 1838. [NRS.S/H]

MANN, JOHN, born 1808, for 24 years was schoolmaster in Baldernock, died 26 January 1858. [Baldernock gravestone, Stirlingshire]

MANSON, DANIEL, schoolmaster in Stirling, dead by 1834. [NRS.S/H]

MANSON, EUPHEMIA, spouse of James Paterson a baker in Stirling, testament, 1793, Comm. Stirling. [NRS]

MANSON, MAY, born 1712, a servant to the family of Dunipace, died 14 December 1804. [Falkirk gravestone, Stirlingshire]

MARSHALL, DAVID, in Roughhaugh, Polmont, Stirlingshire, died in November 1863, brother of James Marshall a farmer in Vienna, Ontario. [NRS.S/H]

MARSHALL, JAMES, and Marion Smith, 1808. [Falkirk gravestone, Stirlingshire]

MARSHALL, JAMES, a farmer in Vienna, Ontario, brother and heir of David Marshall in Roughhaugh, Polmont, Stirlingshire, who died in November 1863. [NRS.S/H]

MARSHALL, JOHN, with his wife, of the Balfron Emigration Society, Stirlingshire, from Greenock aboard the <u>David of London</u> bound for Quebec, Canada, on 19 May 1821, was granted land in Lanark, Upper Canada in 1821. [PAO]

MARSHALL, MARY, born 1771, died on 29 April 1852, wife of Alexander Stein. [Alloa gravestone, Clackmannanshire]

MARSHALL, WILLIAM, from Falkirk, Stirlingshire, a merchant in Jamaica, testament, 1796, Comm. Edinburgh. [NRS]

MARTIN, ALEXANDER, a clerk in Boston, Massachusetts, son and heir of Helen Miller, wife of Robert Martin, a mason in Dunblane, Stirlingshire, who died on 28 April 1883. [NRS.S/H]

MARTIN, JOHN, a music teacher and choir master in Kilmadock in 1856. [SJA.29/8,3D]

MASTERTON, ALEXANDER, master of the <u>William of Kincardine</u> trading between Inverkeithing and Alloa in 1817. [NRS.E504.2.13]

MASTERTON, ROBERT, in Stirling in 1852. [SJA.20/2,4E]

MATHIE, JAMES, of the Alloa Emigration Society, with his wife, five sons and a daughter, from Greenock aboard the <u>David of London</u> bound for Quebec, Canada, on 19 May 1821, was granted land in Lanark, Upper Canada on 10 September 1821. [PAO]

MATHIE, JOHN, a shoemaker in Stirling, married Janet Sharp in 1811, however she absconded with Alexander Thomson of Longstone near Slateford in 1812, a Process of Divorce in 1819. [NRS.CC8.5.37]

MATHIE, ROBERT, a writer and banker in Stirling in 1858. [SJA.28/5.4D]

MATHIESON, Reverend D., son of George Mathieson, [1764-1845], and his wife Janet Ewing, [1764-1857], settled in Montreal, Quebec. [Campsie gravestone, Stirlingshire]

MATHISON, THOMAS, born in 1804, a teacher of mathematics at McNab's school, died on 30 June 1833. [Dollar gravestone, Clackmannanshire]

MATTERS, JOHN, master gunner of Stirling Castle in 1855. [SJA.18/5.3B]

MAXTON, ALEXANDER, born 1794, son of Reverend John Maxton, died in Montreal, Quebec, in 1830. [Alloa gravestone, Clackmannanshire]

MAXWELL, CRAWFORD MAIN, was admitted as a burgess and guildsbrother of Stirling in 1813. [SBR]

MAXWELL, ROBERT WILSON, in Falkirk in 1838. [SJA.26/10,4F]

MAXWELL, WILLIAM B., a glassworker in Alloa, Clackmannanshire, married Ann Tickner, in Edinburgh, 6 December 1838. [SO]

MEFFAN, ALEXANDER, police officer in Dunblane, Stirlingshire, in 1850. [SJA.18/1,4D]

MEIKLE, GEORGE, a millwright in Alloa, Clackmannanshire, a bond, 1790. [NRS.RD2.274.61]

MEIKLEJOHN, JOHN, born 1749, a hewer, died on 2 April 1828, husband of Ann Jeffrey, born 1748, died 30 December 1807. [Alloa gravestone, Clackmannanshire]

MEIKLEJOHN, PETER, in Doune, Stirlingshire, in 1835. [SJA.2/10,4C]

MELDRUM, ALEXANDER, born 1802, manager of the Devon Ironworks, died on 12 July 1835. [Clackmannan gravestone]

MELDRUM, LESLIE, in Clackmannan, a victim of rioting etc, there in 1842. [NRS.AD14.42.339]

MENZIES, ARCHIBALD, born 1774, Major of the 42nd Regiment [The Black Watch], died on 11 July 1854, and his wife Euphemia Menzies, born 1787, died 8 December 1860; parents of Thomas Jack Murray Menzies, who died in New Zealand on 25 December 1888; Alexander Henry Murray Menzies, born 1852, who died in Ceylon on 9 May

1886; Robert Menzies, born 1830, a Lieutenant of the 1st Madras Fusiliers born 1830, died in Bangalore, Mysore, India, on 14 August 1860. [Polmont gravestone, Stirlingshire]

MENZIES, WILLIAM, in Sheriffmuir, Stirlingshire, in 1862. [SJA.15/8,4C]

MERCER, JAMES, a joiner in Dundas, Canada, grandson and heir of James Mercer, a labourer in Catacraig, Bannockburn, Stirlingshire, who died on 9 August 1853. [NRS.S/H]

MERCER, JOHN, master of the Eliza of Kincardine trading between Alloa and Hamburg, Germany, in 1816. [NRS.E504.2.13]

MERRYLEES, ROBERT, born 1818, for twenty-seven years a missionary in Balfron, died in 1885, husband of Janet McAlpine. [Balfron gravestone, Stirlingshire]

METHVEN, ALEXANDER, a weaver, was admitted as a burgess of Stirling in 1804. [SBR]

MILL, WILLIAM, an ironmonger in Falkirk, Stirlingshire, in 1860. [SJA.24/2,4D]

MILLER, ALEXANDER, with his wife Agnes Moir, daughter Janet, and son Peter, in Arnprior, Stirlingshire, emigrated via Greenock to Montreal, Quebec aboard the brig Niagara, Captain Hamilton, in 1825, settled in McNab, Bathurst, Upper Canada. [SG]

MILLER, DAVID, and his wife Jean Aitken, parents of Alexander Millar, born 1853, died in Hinsdale, New Hampshire, on 11 April 1925. [Stirling gravestone]

MILLER, DAVID, a mason, died on 20 May 1819. [Dollar gravestone, Clackmannanshire]

MILLER, JAMES, son of John Miller a farmer in Polmont, Stirlingshire, was educated at Glasgow University in 1809, emigrated to America. [MAGU]

MILLER, JAMES, from Falkirk, Stirlingshire, a theological student in 1811, emigrated to America. [UPC]

MILLER, JAMES, born 1793 in Dunmore, Stirlingshire, emigrated via London to Wilmington, North Carolina, in September 1815, was naturalised in Cumberland County, N.C., in March 1826. [NCA. CR029.301.16]

MILLER, JAMES, from Stirling, a merchant in Charleston, South Carolina, was drowned in the wreck of the Rose in Bloom in August 1806. [AJ.3075][GM.76.1168]

MILLER, JAMES, messenger at arms, Stirling, 1849. [POD]

MILLER, JAMES, the Danish Consul in Alloa, Clackmannanshire, in 1849. [SJA.23/3, 4f]

MILLER, JANE, youngest daughter of the late John Miller from Stirlingshire, married George De Blois from Halifax, New Brunswick, in Bathurst, N.B., on 24 October 1838. [Nova Scotian, 25.10.1838]

MILLER, JOHN, the elder, born 1762 in Stirlingshire, died in St John, New Brunswick, on 4 October 1828. [Miramichi Mercury, 7.10.1828]

MILLER, JOHN, of the Dunblane Weaving Factory, Stirlingshire, in 1840. [SJA.24/1.4E]

MILLER, WILLIAM, from Falkirk, Stirlingshire, a divinity student in 1814, emigrated to America. [AUPC]

MILLER, WILLIAM, born 1831, son of Peter Miller, [1799-1861], a farmer, and his wife Mary Whyte, [1782-1836], was drowned in the Ruebin River, New Zealand, on 30 May 1862. [Holy Rude gravestone, Stirling]

MILLER, WILLIAM REID, born 1834, son of James Miller and his wife Margaret Reid, was drowned in Jacob's River, New Zealand, on 1 May 1870. [Logie gravestone, Stirling]

MILNE, WILLIAM, born in Falkirk, Stirlingshire, son of Alexander Milne, a W.S., and his wife Sarah Swan, a Lieutenant in the Royal Navy, settled In Canada, died in Ancaster, Upper Canada, on 27 February 1825. [DF]

MITCHELL, ELIZA, born 1827, daughter of William Mitchell, and the widow of Robert Schaw Miller in Montreal, Quebec, died in Alloa, Clackmannanshire, on 30 August 1863. [Greenside gravestone, Alloa]

MITCHELL, G., master of the William Mitchell of Alloa from Leith with passengers bound for Australia on 7 December 1838, landed in Hobart on 17 June 1839, [Colonial Record, Launceston, 24.6.1839]; from Leith to New South Wales in 1839, [LCL.27.2700]; from Leith with 45 passengers bound for Australia on 21 July1841, landed in Melbourne on 15 December 1841. [EEC.20214]

MITCHELL, JOHN, in Graham Street, Doune, Master of the Lodge St James number 171 in 1801. [brother of William Mitchell of Bushy Park, Jamaica] [DHN.iii]

MITCHELL, JOHN, born 1767 in Falkirk, a sailor, an inmate of William Simpson's Asylum for 3 years, died there on 14 May 1841. [Plean gravestone, Stirlingshire]

MITCHELL, JOHN, a gun-moulder in Carron, Stirlingshire, marred Ann McLeish, at Mungall Mill on 19 January 1843. [SO]

MITCHELL, JOHN JAMES, in Welsford Mills, Pictou, Nova Scotia, grandson and heir of James Mitchell sr. in Gargunnock, Stirlingshire, who died on 25 December 1855. [NRS.S/H]

MITCHELL, MAGDALENE, born 1838, daughter of James Mitchell, [1800-1872], and his wife Elizabeth Thomson, [1800-1843], died in Barony, New Brunswick, on 25 January 1872. [Larbert gravestone, Stirlingshire]

MITCHELL, MARGARET, in Doune, Stirlingshire, was accused of the theft of cotton, she petitioned for banishment, 1791. [NRS.JC26.1791.14]

MITCHELL, Sir THOMAS, born 15 June 1792 in Craigend, Strathblane, or Grangemouth, Stirlingshire, son of John Mitchell and his wife Janet Wilson, Surveyor General of New South Wales in 1827 later an Australian explorer, died 1855. [DNB]

MITCHELL, THOMAS, eldest son of ..... Mitchell the harbour-master of Grangemouth, Stirlingshire, a Lieutenant of the Rifle Brigade, married Mary Blunt, eldest daughter of Lieutenant General Blunt, in Lisbon, Portugal, in 1818. [SM.82.587]CS284.191]

MITCHELL, WILLIAM, born 1781, a merchant and shipowner, died on 17 February 1854, husband of Janet Wingate, died on 20 August 1835, parents of William Mitchell, the tacksman of Alloa Mills, who died on 11 May 1838. [Alloa gravestone, Clackmannanshire]

MOFFAT, JOHN, jr., was admitted as a burgess and guilds-brother of Stirling in 1811. [SBR]

MOIR, ARCHIBALD, a banker in Alloa, married Susan Main or Baird at Marshill, Alloa, 14 April 1854. [SO]

MOIR, BENJAMIN, born 1784 in Stirling, was a labourer residing in Green Street, Glasgow, in 1820, was exiled to Australia in 1821 for his part in the Uprising of 1820, his wife and two daughters joined him in 1822, he was granted a Certificate of Freedom in 1827, he settled in Sydney, New South Wales. [TSR]

MOIR, BENJAMIN, a maltman, was admitted as a burgess and guilds-brother of Stirling in 1811. [SBR]

MOIR, JAMES, formerly a writer in Alloa, Clackmannanshire, later in Kingston, Jamaica, by 1881. [NRS]

MOIR, JOHN, a surgeon, married Ann Lorn, in Grangemouth, Stirlingshire, on 14 June 1838. [SO]

MOIR, JOHN, jr., a Writer to the Signet, was admitted as a burgess and guilds-brother of Stirling in 1801. [SBR]

MOIR, ..., agent of the Commercial Bank of Scotland in Alloa, Clackmannanshire, in 1849. [POD]

MONCRIEFF, CHARLES, a cordiner, was admitted as a burgess of Stirling in 1804. [SBR]

MONTEITH, CHARLES, a mechanic, was admitted as a burgess of Stirling in 1811. [SBR]

MONTEITH, JAMES, son of Walter Monteith of Keep, died in Jamaica on 18 September 1798, his widow Amelia, born 1767, died in Lympstone, Devon, on 20 April 1833. [AJ.2661] [GM.103.476]

MONTEITH, JAMES, agent of the Clydesdale Bank in Stirling in 1849. [POD]

MONTEITH, JOHN, born 1812, died 11 June 1889, husband of Isabella Baird, born 1821, died 15 March 1884. [Falkirk gravestone, Stirlingshire]

MONTGOMERY, W., a clock and watchmaker in Falkirk around 1850. [OSC.108]

MOODIE, Reverend, chaplain of the Clackmannan Volunteers, was admitted as a burgess and guilds-brother of Dunfermline, Fife, on 24 February 1802. [DM]

MORRISON, JAMES, born 1849 in Alva, Clackmannanshire, son of James Morrison, [1800-1867], a manufacturer, and his wife Margaret Paton, [1810-1878], died on 19 December 1868 and was buried in the British Cemetery, Funchal, Madeira. [Alva gravestone] [ARM]

MORRISON, JANE, fourth daughter of Robert Morrison and his wife Christina Duncan, died in Winton, Australia, on 30 June 1885. [Campsie gravestone, Stirlingshire]

MORRISON, PETER, a mason in Doune, Stirlingshire, Master of the Lodge St James number 171 from 1836-1837. [DHN.iii]

MORRISON, RACHEL, in Stirling, testament, 1795, Comm. Stirling. [NRS]

MORRISON, ROBERT, a mason in Doune, Stirlingshire, Master of the Lodge St James number 171 from 1826-1827. [DHN.iii]

MORRISON, THOMAS, master of the <u>Nancy of Stirling</u> trading between Leith and Alloa in 1816. [NRS.E504.2.13]

MORRISON, THOMAS, born 1801, died 23 March 1839, husband of Barbara Porteous, born 1802, died on 6 November 1882. [Alloa gravestone, Clackmannanshire]

MORRISON, WILLIAM, 1801, husband of Janet Black, 1828, parents of Colin Morrison 'lately from Jamaica'. [Falkirk gravestone, Stirlingshire]

MORTON, or NICOL, FRANCES, in Falkirk, Stirlingshire, died 1 July 1855, mother of Robert Nicol a ship carpenter in America. [NRS.S/H]

MOUAT, WILLIAM, Land Surveyor of Customs at Alloa in 1816. [NRS.E504.2.13]

MOUBRAY, JOHN, Captain of the Clackmannan Volunteers, was admitted as a burgess and guilds-brother of Dunfermline, Fife, on 22 February 1804. [DM]

MOWART, ARCHIBALD, was admitted as a burgess and guilds-brother of Stirling in 1808. [SBR]

MOWBRAY, MARGARET, wife of John Anderson in Chicago, Illinois, cousin and heir of Elizabeth Mowbray in Airth, Stirlingshire, who died in September 1854. [NRS.S/H]

MUDIE, THOMAS, a clock and watch maker in Balfron, Stirlingshire, in 1798. [OSC.108]

MUIR, GEORGE, born 1824, son of George Muir and his wife Janet Houston, died in Greymouth, New Zealand, on 6 December 1873. [Holy Rude gravestone, Stirling]

MUIRHEAD, AGNES, in Falkirk, Stirlingshire, widow of Dougald Stewart a merchant in Jamaica, testament, 8 March 1793, Comm. Glasgow. [NRS]

MUIRHEAD, JOHN, a truckman in Lubec, Washington County, Maine, son and heir of John Muirhead in Bankhead, Denny, Stirlingshire, who died in December 1839, also, to his grandfather John Muirhead there, who died in December 1839. [NRS.S/H]

MUIRHEAD, W., messenger at arms, Denny, Stirlingshire, 1849. [POD]

MUIRHEAD, WILLIAM, a writer in Stirling, testament, 1800, Comm. Stirling. [NRS]

MUNGAL, ROBERT, a maltman, was admitted as a burgess and guildsbrother of Stirling in 1812. [SBR]

MUNNOCH, ALEXANDER, a mechanic, was admitted as a burgess of Stirling in 1820. [SBR]

MUNRO, JAMES, born 1843, son of William Munro, [1817-1900], and his wife Janet McCrostie, [1817-1901], died in St Louis, Missouri, on 13 June 1868. [Alva gravestone, Clackmannanshire]

MURDOCH, ARCHIBALD, son of James Murdoch and his wife Beatrix Campbell, at Bridge of Teith, Doune, Stirlingshire, died in Jamaica in December 1800. [Kilmadock gravestone, Perthshire]

MURDOCH, JAMES, a slater and a feuar in Doune, Stirlingshire, Master of the Lodge St James number 171 in 1844-1845. [DHN.iii]

MURDOCH, JAMES, married Robina Galbraith, in Hobart, Tasmania, Australia, 16 November 1837. [SO]

MURDOCH, JANE, born 1816, wife of James Forrester, died Oamaru, New Zealand, on 16 June 1881. [Gargunnock gravestone, Stirlingshire]

MURDOCH, THOMAS, a shoemaker, was admitted as a burgess of Stirling in 1811. [SBR]

MURRAY, ARCHIBALD, in Alloa, Clackmannanshire, applied to settle in Canada on 29 February 1815. [NRS.RH9]

MURRAY, Reverend DAVID, was admitted as a burgess and guildsbrother of Stirling in 1814. [SBR]

MURRAY, DAVIDSON MUNRO, third son of William Murray late of HM Civil Service, grandson of Alexander Bruce MD in Edinburgh and Barbados, nephew of David Bruce of Kennet, Clackmannanshire, died in Canada in 1852. [FJ.1004]

MURRAY, JAMES, married Anne Waugh, eldest daughter of Patrick Waugh, Arbuthnott Cottage, Stirlingshire, and of Dromilly Estate, Trelawney, Jamaica, on Georgia Estate, Trelawney, Jamaica, on 24 September 1840. [AJ.4848]

MURRAY, JAMES, born 1843, died in Maryborough, Australia, on 20 October 1883. [Kincardine, Blairdrummond, gravestone]

MURRAY, ROBERT, a skipper on Carronshore, testament, 1790, Comm. Stirling. [NRS]

MURRIE, JOHN, agent of the National Bank of Scotland in Stirling, in 1849. [POD]

NAPIER, HELEN, wife of J. Forrester in Stirling Castle, dead by 1816. [NRS.S/H]

NAPIER, ROBERT, a shoemaker, son of William Napier, was admitted as a burgess of Stirling in 1845. [SBR]

NAPIER, WILLIAM, a cordiner, was admitted as a burgess of Stirling in 1804. [SBR]

NAPIER, WILLIAM, son of Alexander Napier, was admitted as a burgess and guilds-brother of Stirling in 1846. [SBR]

NEILSON, CHRISTIAN, born 1748, died 14 March 1792, wife of John Mackie, a merchant on Carronshore. [Falkirk gravestone, Stirlingshire]

NEILSON, JOSEPH, son of William Neilson, [1803-1898], and his wife Mary Finlayson, [1811-1898], died in America on 5 November 1871. [Dunblane gravestone, Stirlingshire]

NEILSON, MARGARET, born 1800, second wife of James McLuchlan, died in Galt, Ontario, on 12 March 1822. [Buchlyvie gravestone, Stirlingshire]

NEILSON, THOMAS, in St Mary's, Jamaica, second son of Thomas Neilson a merchant in Falkirk, Stirlingshire, in 1799, [NRS.CS18.706.52]; died in Glasgow in February 1800, testament, Comm. Glasgow. [NRS.CC9.7.77]

NEILSON, THOMAS, a farmer in Balgair, Stirlingshire, a deed in favour of Andrew Crawford a writer in Stirling on 12 November 1838. [NRS.GD22.1.510]

NELSON, DAVID, born in Stirlingshire, emigrated to America in 1825, was naturalised in Newberry, South Carolina, on 15 April 1829. [SCA]

NESS, WILLIAM, was admitted as a burgess of Stirling in 1810. [SBR]

NEY, PETER STEWART, born 1787 in Stirlingshire, was naturalised in Marlborough County, South Carolina, in March 1820. [SCA]

NICOL, ANDREW, a mariner in Australia, son of John Nicol and his wife Elizabeth Key in Carronshore, in 1858. [NRS.S/H]

NICOL, BENJAMIN, a wheelwright in Falkirk, Stirlingshire, dead by 1837, father of James Nicol in Grenada. [NRS.S/H]

NICOL, J., late an officer in the Service of the East India Company, died on 26 September 1784, husband of Mary Stephen, died 27 December 1816. [Alloa gravestone, Clackmannanshire]

NICHOL, JOHN, with his wife, four sons, and a daughter, of the Balfron Emigration Society, Stirlingshire, from Greenock aboard the David of London bound for Quebec, Canada, on 19 May 1821, was granted land in Ramsay, Upper Canada, on 7 August 1821. [PAO]

NICOL, ROBERT, a ship's carpenter in America, son and heir of Frances Morton or Nicol in Falkirk, Stirlingshire, who died on 1 July 1855. [NRS.S/H]

NIMMO, ROBERT, in Falkirk, Stirlingshire, dead by 1817, son of William Nimmo a merchant in Virginia. [NRS.S/H]

NIMMO, WILLIAM, died in St Kilda, Australia, on 30 July 1873. [Logie, Stirling, gravestone]

NISBET, GEORGE, a mechanic, was admitted as a burgess of Stirling in 1804. [SBR]

NISBET, SAMUEL, born 1831, died in Australia on 4 June 1914. [Baldernock gravestone, Stirlingshire]

NORRIES, JOHN, was found guilty of assault and theft, sentenced to 14 years transportation for 14 years to the colonies, at Stirling in 1815. [NRS.GD1.959]

OATT, FRANCIS, in Doune, Stirlingshire, Master of the Lodge St James number 171 from 1802 until 1803, also from 1812 to 1813, and 1816-1817. [DHN.ii1854]; was admitted as a burgess of Stirling in 1818. [SBR]

OATT, or CAMERON, ..., died in New York on 14 September 1854. [SO]

OATTS, WILLIAM, a weaver, was admitted as a burgess of Stirling in 1851. [SBR]

OGILVIE, ROBERT, was admitted as a burgess and guilds-brother of Stirling in 1818. [SBR]

OLIPHANT, EBENEZER, from Port Philip, Victoria, Australia, married Agnes McLaurin, at Guldees, on 15 April 1847. [SO]

OLIPHANT, LILIAS BALFOUR, born 1769, died on 16 January 1852. [Alloa gravestone, Clackmannanshire]

ORR, JAMES RAMSAY, born 1807, a merchant in Montreal, Quebec, died on 16 March 1852. [Stirling gravestone]

ORR, THOMAS WILLIAM, born 1847, son of James Orr and his wife Martha Thomson, died in Blenheim, New Zealand on 8 April 1922. [Holy Rude gravestone, Stirling]

OSBURN, WILLIAM, was admitted as a burgess and guilds-brother of Stirling in 1800. [SBR]

OSWALD, ANDREW, from Grangemouth, Stirlingshire, and Charlotte Snook, third daughter of Robert Snook in St John's, Newfoundland, were married in Halifax, Nova Scotia, on 19 February 1838. [Acadian Recorder, 30 July 187323.2.1838]

OSWALD, JOHN, and Mary Manuel, 1820. [Falkirk gravestone, Stirlingshire]

OSWALD, MARGARET, wife of John Burns in Canada West, was heir of Mary Oswald, wife of William Wilson in Larbert, Stirlingshire, later in Belfast, Ireland, died in February 1857. [NRS.S/H]

OSWALD, PETER, was admitted as a burgess of Stirling in 1828. [SBR]

OWEN, JOSEPH, was admitted as a burgess of Stirling in 1846. [SBR]

PARLANE, JAMES, a maltman, was admitted as a burgess of Stirling in 1831. [SBR]

PATERSON, ALEXANDER, a carrier in Stirling, testament, 1799, Comm. Stirling. [NRS]

PATERSON, ALEXANDER, MD, born on 16 June 1822, a physician in Bridge of Allan for over 50 years, died on 22 April 1898. [Logie Old gravestone, Stirlingshire]

PATERSON, JAMES, a nailer in St Ninian's, Stirlingshire, was dead by 1851, father of John Paterson a nailer in Illinois. [NRS.S/H]

PATERSON, JOHN, born in 1807, underground coal manager of the Alloa Coal Company, died on 11 January 1893. [Clackmannan gravestone]

PATERSON, WILLIAM, a merchant in Stirling, a merchant in 1810. [NRS.CS96.3358]

PATERSON, WILLIAM, a clock and watchmaker in Falkirk around 1830. [OSC.108]

PATON, ANDREW, tenant in Cambus Mill, a thief, was sentenced at Stirling to be transported for life on 15 April 1789. [AJ.2156]

PATON, or FULTON, CATHERINE, in Dollar, Clackmannanshire, was dead by 1854. [NRS.SH]

PATON, J. and D., in Tillicoultry, Clackmannanshire, victims of theft and reset in 1852. [NRS.AD14.14.52.373]

PATON, JOHN, a maltman and brewer in Stirling, testament, 1790, Comm. Stirling. [NRS]

PATON, JOHN, a weaver, was admitted as a burgess of Stirling in 1802. [SBR]

PATON, WILLIAM, a writer in Stirling, brother and heir of John Paton in Jamaica, in 1838. [NRS.S/H]

PATON, WILLIAM, in Clackmannan, a victim of rioting etc, there in 1842. [NRS.AD14.42.339]

PATTEN, JOHN, son of James Patten, was admitted as a burgess and guilds-brother of Stirling in 1831. [SBR]

PATRICK, Reverend WILLIAM, born in Kilsyth, Stirlingshire, a minister in Lockerbie, Dumfries-shire, emigrated to Miramachi, New Brunswick, in 1815, minister at Merigomish, Nova Scotia, from 1815 until his death on 25 November 1844. [HPC]

PAUL, JESSIE, daughter of David Paul, [1783-1860], and his wife Margaret Nimmo, [1797-1880], wife of William Nimmo, died in St Kilda, Australia, on 9 June 1867. [Logie, Stirling, gravestone]

PAUL, WILLIAM, a maltman, was admitted as a burgess of Stirling in 1810. [SBR]

PAUL, WILLIAM NIMMO, died in St Kilda, Australia, on 30 July 1873. [Logie gravestone, Stirling]

PEARSON, DAVID, was admitted as a burgess and guilds-brother of Stirling in 1804. [SBR]

PEARSON, HUGH, of Myrecairnie, was admitted as a burgess and guilds-brother of Stirling in 1820. [SBR]

PEAT, THOMAS, a hammerman, was admitted as a burgess of Stirling in 1817. [SBR]

PEDDIE, ANDREW, a hammerman, was admitted as a burgess of Stirling in 1801. [SBR]

PEDDIE, GEORGE, a hammerman, son of Andrew Peddie, was admitted as a burgess of Stirling in 1849. [SBR]

PEDDIE, JAMES, a watchmaker in Stirling, married Elisabeth McDonald, in Stirling, 4 January 1849. [SO]

PENNIE, JAMES, a mechanic, was admitted as a burgess of Stirling in 1832. [SBR]

PETER, DAVID, a mechanic, was admitted as a burgess of Stirling in 1836. [SBR]

PICKEN, ANDREW, was admitted as a burgess and guilds-brother of Stirling in 1853. [SBR]

PILLING, ROBERT, was admitted as a burgess and guilds-brother of Stirling in 1802. [SBR]

POLLOCK, ALEXANDER, a weaver, was admitted as a burgess of Stirling in 1824. [SBR]

POLLOCK, ARCHIBALD, a weaver, was admitted as a burgess of Stirling in 1802. [SBR]

POPE, JAMES R., messenger at arms, Falkirk, Stirlingshire, 1849. [POD]

PORTEOUS, ARCHIBALD, in Alva, Clackmannanshire, a victim of theft and reset in 1852. [NRS.AD14.52.373]

PRENTICE, JAMES, was admitted as a burgess and guilds-brother of Stirling in 1815. [SBR]

PRENTICE, JOHN, a mechanic, was admitted as a burgess of Stirling in 1826. [SBR]

PRESTON, JAMES, in Stirling, applied to settle in Canada on 1 March 1815. [NRS.RH9]

PRIMROSE, DAVID, a skipper in Tulliallan, an inventory, 1814, Comm. Dunblane. [NRS]

PRINGLE, GEORGE, a clock and watchmaker in Denny, Stirlingshire, in 181. [OSC.108]

PROP, GRIZZEL, servant to the Colvin family of Denovan, died in 1807. [Falkirk gravestone, Stirlingshire]

PROVAN, MATTHEW, son of John Provan a manufacturer in Kilsyth, Stirlingshire, was educated at Glasgow University in 1802, died in Natchez, Mississippi, on 4 October1821. [MAGU]

PURVIS, JOHN, a hammerman, was admitted as a burgess of Stirling in 1807. [SBR]

RAE, JOHN, born 1772, son of Edward Rae in St Ninian's, Stirlingshire, was educated at Glasgow University, minister of St Andrew's from Nassau, New Providence, Bahama Islands from 1797 until 1816, died in Stirling on 26 February 1821. [UPC] [F.7.667]

RAE, JOHN, a baker, was admitted as a burgess of Stirling in 1800. [SBR]

REA, SAMUEL, born 1817, a grocer and publican in Grahamston, Falkirk, Stirlingshire, was accused of theft and reset in 1852. [NRS.AD14.52.373]

RAEBURN, JAMES, master of the Latona of Kincardine trading between Alloa and St Petersburg, Russia, in 1817. [NRS.E504.2.13]

RALSTON, ALEXANDER, born 1755 in Falkirk, a carrier in St Ninian's, Stirling, emigrated to New England in 1773, died in Keene, New Hampshire, in 1810. [ImmNE.161][NRS.CS17.1.24/245]

RALSTON, ALEXANDER, was admitted as a burgess and guilds-brother of Stirling in 1822. [SBR]

RALSTON, JAMES, a cordiner, was admitted as a burgess of Stirling in 1804. [SBR]

RALSTON, PETER, a tanner in St Ninian's, Stirling, emigrated to North America before 1806. [NRS.CS17.1.25/37]

RAMSAY, EBENEZER, born 1815, son of Ebenezer Ramsay and his wife Margaret Flint in Alloa, Clackmannanshire, died in Jamaica on 3 December 1858. [Alloa gravestone]

RAMSAY, JOHN, born 1773, a distiller from Clackmannan, was naturalised in South Carolina on 23 January 1804. [NARA.M1183.1]

RAMSAY, ROBERT, a hammerman, was admitted as a burgess of Stirling in 1802. [SBR]

RAMSAY, THOMAS, a maltman in Alloa, Clackmannanshire, disposed of a tenement in Alloa to John Francis Erskine of Mar in 1797. [NRS.GD124.1.908]

RAMSAY, THOMAS, a skinner, was admitted as a burgess of Stirling in 1802. [SBR]

RAMSAY, ..., agent of the Western Bank of Scotland in Alloa, Clackmannanshire, in 1849. [POD]

RANKINE, MARY, daughter of the late William Rankine in Lone Ridge, Stirlingshire, married James Dawson a merchant, in Pictou, Nova Scotia, on 8 December 1818. [Free Press, 22 December 1818]

RANKINE, WILLIAM, born 1784, a merchant from Stirlingshire, died in Pictou, Nova Scotia, on 30 December 1827. [Acadian Recorder, 12.1.1828]

RANKIN, WILLIAM, a cork-cutter, was admitted as a burgess of Stirling in 1833. [SBR]

RANKIN, the Misses, in Falkirk, a deed, 23 June 1841. [NRS.RD29.3.23]

RATTRAY, ANDREW, in Grandview, Washington County, USA, brother and heir of William Rattray a builder in Falkirk, Stirlingshire, who died 16 October 1865. [NRS.S/H]

RATTRAY, CHARLES, a weaver and a maltman, was admitted as a burgess of Stirling in 1801. [SBR]

RAY, ANDREW, a brewer in Alloa, Clackmannanshire, trustee for James Graham, a maltster and corn merchant in Alloa in 1831. [NRS.CS96.233]

REDDIE, DAVID, was admitted as a burgess and guilds-brother of Stirling in 1822. [SBR]

REDDIE, DAVID, [1821-1898], and his wife Jane Spittall, [1819-1890], parents of John Oatts Reddie, born 1859, who died at Prince Rupert, British Columbia, on 28 August 1912. Holy Rude gravestone, Stirling]

REDDIE, THOMAS HENDERSON, a brass-founder in Stirling, married Elizabeth Gregory, in Leeds, 10 June 1852. [SO]

REID, HUGH, born 1812 in Alloa, Clackmannanshire, master of the schooner Elizabeth, died in St John, New Brunswick, on 5 January 1838. [New Brunswick Courier, 6.1.1838]

REID, ROBERT, born 1804, died 1872, husband of Margaret Murdoch, born 1803, died 1901, parents of a son who died in Australia in 1881. [Erskine gravestone, Stirling]

REID, ROBERT GALBRAITH, son of James Reid, was admitted as a burgess and guilds-brother of Stirling in 1849. [SBR]

RENNY, GEORGE, of Birkhill, Stirlingshire, died on 14 November 1820 in Port Glasgow, [Acadian Recorder, 17.11.1820]

RENNIE, JEAN, died 19 August 1831. [Falkirk gravestone, Stirlingshire]

RENNIE, JOHN, in Allanfauld, Kilsyth, Stirlingshire, was a victim of cattle stealing in 1837. [NRS.AD14.37.528]

RENNY, MARGARET, daughter of George Renny in Falkirk, Stirlingshire, died in Edinburgh on 24 March 1819. [Acadian Recorder, 22.5.1819]

RENNIE, JOHN, born 1781, died in Mungalland, Falkirk, on 17 September 1825. [Larbert gravestone, Stirlingshire]

RENNIE, WILLIAM, in Grahamstone, born 1745, died 11 February 1825. [Falkirk gravestone, Stirlingshire]

RHIND, JAMES NATHANIEL, Lieutenant Colonel of the Loyal Stirling Volunteers, was admitted as a burgess and guilds-brother of Dunfermline, Fife, on 17 July 1804. [DM]

RHIND, WILLIAM, of Wester Livilands, a merchant in Stirling, testament, 1793, Comm. Stirling. [NRS]

RICHARDSON, JOHN, a maltster from Stirling, later in New York, heir to Major James Livingstone, 1798. [NRS.GD1.660.1]

RICHARDSON, JOHN, a baker, was admitted as a burgess of Stirling in 1848. [SBR]

RICHARDSON, WILLIAM, a clock and watchmaker in Balfron, Stirlingshire, in 1828. [OSC.108]

RIDDELL, JAMES, was admitted as a burgess and guilds-brother of Stirling in 1827. [SBR]

RIDDELL, JAMES, a surgeon, married Mary Campbell, in Denny, Stirlingshire, 6 May 1847. [SO]

RISK, WILLIAM, born 1801, a ship's carpenter, died on 9 December 1851, husband of Elizabeth Hall, born 1805, died 11 July 1865, [Alloa gravestone, Clackmannanshire]

RITCHIE, JAMES, born 1819, son of John Ritchie and his wife Margaret Henderson in Logie, Stirlingshire, died in Jamaica on 11 November 1861. [Logie gravestone]

RITCHIE, WILLIAM, in West Quarter of Tillicoultry Clackmannanshire, was a victim of housebreaking in 1837. [NRS.AD14.37.208]

ROBB, JAMES, from Stirling, a resident of Charleston, S.C., was naturalised in South Carolina on 24 May 1830. [NARA.M1183.1]

ROB, RALPH, was admitted as a burgess and guilds-brother of Stirling in 1810. [SBR]

ROBB, WILLIAM, born in 1749, a farmer in Manor, died on 17 June 1818, husband of Lillias Jaffrey, born in 1756, died on 12 August 1820. [Logie Old gravestone, Stirlingshire]

ROBB, WILLIAM, of Duthieston, eldest son of John Robb the Sheriff of Dunblane, Stirlingshire, residing in Jamaica, was granted lands in Dunblane on 2 June 1818. [NRS.RGS.157.46.102]

ROBERTSON, JAMES, a shoemaker, was admitted as a burgess of Stirling in 1830. [SBR]

ROBERTSON, JAMES, in Clackmannan, a victim of rioting etc, there in 1842. [NRS.AD14.42.339]

ROBERTSON, JAMES, a butcher, was admitted as a burgess of Stirling in 1847. [SBR]

ROBERTSON, JAMES, a tailor from Denny, Stirlingshire, later in Paris, Canada, a mandate, 1852. [NRS.67.49.28/179]

ROBERTSON, JOHN, and his wife Ann Shorthouse, were parents of Robert Robertson, born 1855, died in Hamilton, Tasmania, Australia, on 10 March 1888. [Holy Rude gravestone, Stirling]

ROBERTSON, JOHN, a grocer in St Ninian's, Stirling, married Margaret Drysdale, at Craigforth Mills, 23 December 1852. [SO]

ROBERTSON, JOSEPH, session clerk of the Free Church in Dunblane, Stirlingshire, a petition, 1 May 1845. [NRS.GD112.51.189]

ROBERTSON, MICHAEL, agent of the British Linen Company in Balfron, Stirlingshire, in 1849. [POD]

ROBERTSON, PETER, a seaman in Condie, Stirlingshire, testament, 1819, Comm. Stirling. [NRS]

ROBERTSON, THOMAS, born in 1784, a farmer in Cornton, died on 27 April 1856, husband of Margaret Stirling, born 1779, died on 7 January 1815. [Logie Old gravestone, Stirlingshire]

ROBERTSON, THOMAS, son of Thomas Robertson, was admitted as a burgess and guilds-brother of Stirling in 1846. [SBR]

ROBERTSON, THOMAS, born 24 November 1821, ordained 28 September 1843, first minister of Dunipace Free Church, died 5 March 1898, husband of Elizabeth Greig, born 1819, died 31 March 1902. [Falkirk gravestone, Stirlingshire]

ROBERTSON, WILLIAM, a planter on Lejuan Island, Essequibo, a bond in favour of Duncan Glassford of Tillicoultry, Clackmannanshire, subscribed in Demerara in 1812. [NRS.TD5.129.194]

ROBERTSON, WILLIAM, a wine merchant in Stirling, married Catherine Graham, in Stirling, 17 October 1844. [SO]

ROBISON, WALTER, born in May 1726, settled in Jamaica, died in February 1793. [Strathblane gravestone, Stirlingshire]

RODGERS, EDWARD BAIN, a minister in Toronto, Ontario, son and heir of James Rodgers in Kincardine-on-Forth, who died 4 March 1871. [NRS.S/H]

RONALDS, JOHN, born 1792 in Falkirk, Stirlingshire, a pilot, died aboard the Sceptre at Bathurst, New Brunswick, on 13 May 1835. [New Brunswick Royal Gazette, 24.6.1835]

ROSS, ANDREW, fourth son of Hugh Ross of Kerse, died in Berbice on 26 September 1820. [BM.8.482]

ROSS, CHARLES, a mechanic, was admitted as a burgess of Stirling in 1844. [SBR]

ROSS, JAMES, a shoemaker in Stirling, testament, 1794, Comm. Stirling. [NRS]

ROSS, JOHN, a mechanic, was admitted as a burgess of Stirling in 1850. [SBR]

ROWAT, DAVID, a farmer in Campsie, Stirlingshire, was dead by 1845, father of John Rowat in Canada. [NRS.S/H]

ROY JAMES, born 1799, son of Alexander Roy a farmer in Denny, Stirlingshire, was educated at Glasgow University in 1808, emigrated to Canada in 1827, a minister in Dumfries and Beverley, Canada West, died on 15 May 1852. [MAGU]

ROY, PETER, born 1812, son of John Roy and his wife Mary Davidson in Balquhairn, Logie, died in Pittsfield, Massachusetts, on 24 December 1840. [Logie gravestone, Stirlingshire]

ROY, ..., a Lieutenant of the Clackmannan Volunteers, was admitted as a burgess and guilds-brother of Dunfermline, Fife, on 24 February 1804. [DM]

RUNCEMAN, ALEXANDER, was admitted as a burgess and guilds-brother of Stirling in 1819. [SBR]

RUSSELL, JAMES, a weaver in Longcroft Burn, Denny, Stirlingshire, died 25 May 1814, father of Robert Russell in Porter's Hill, Canada West. [NRS.S/H.1870]

RUSSELL, JAMES, jr., agent of the Clydesdale Bank in Falkirk, Stirlingshire, in 1849. [POD]

RUSSELL, JOHN, born 1740, minister in Stirling from 1799 until his death in 1817. [F.4.326]

RUSSELL, JOHN, born 1745, a watch and clockmaker in Falkirk from 1770 until his death in 1817. [OSC.108]

RUSSELL, WILLIAM, in Graham's Road, Falkirk, Stirlingshire, was dead by 1860, brother of John Russell in Kingston, New York. [NRS.S/H]

St GEORGE, Miss......, daughter of Colonel St George, and grand daughter of John Callander of Craigforth, married S. B. Raffington, from Jamaica, in St Pancras, London, in 1817. [S.24.17]

SALMON, HENRY, agent of the Commercial Bank of Scotland in Falkirk, Stirlingshire, in 1849. [POD]

SALMON, ISABELLA PATERSON, married John Rose Bell, a merchant in Ceylin, in Falkirk, Stirlingshire, 13 October 1853. [SO]

SANDERS, JAMES, Captain of the Clackmannan Volunteers, was admitted as a burgess and guilds-brother of Dunfermline, Fife, on 24 February 1804. [DM]

SANGSTER, WILLIAM, a mariner from Stirlingshire, was naturalised in South Carolina, on 27 October 1797. [NARA.M1183.1]

SAWER, JAMES, Quartermaster of the Stirling Volunteers, was a burgess and guilds-brother of Dunfermline on 17 July 1804. [DM]

SAWERS, JOHN, of Bellfield, born 1760, 'late of Jamaica', died on 8 November 1839. [Stirling gravestone]

SAWERS, JOHN, agent of the Edinburgh and Glasgow Bank in Stirling in 1849. [POD]

SAWYER, WILLIAM, from Stirling, settled in Jamaica around 1776, died there in 1819. [S.145.19] [EA]

SCHOFIELD, WILLIA, a weaver, was admitted as a burgess of Stirling in 1839. [SBR]

SCLANDERS, JAMES, a skipper in Grangemouth, Stirlingshire, a testament, 1810, Comm. Stirling. [NRS]

SCOBBIE, ROBERT, born 1798, died on 18 November 1872, husband of Ann Wright, born 1790, died 28 August 1852, [Alloa gravestone, Clackmannanshire]

SCONCE, ROBERT, son of Robert Sconce, was admitted as a burgess and guilds-brother of Stirling in 1831. [SBR]

SCOTLAND, JOHN, a shipmaster in Tulliallan, Stirlingshire, an inventory, 1805, Comm. Dunblane. [NRS.CC6.W62]

SCOTLAND, JOHN, died on 25 March 1861, husband of Margaret Drysdale who died on 3 November 1853. [Alva gravestone, Clackmannanshire]

SCOTLAND, WILLIAM, a shipmaster in Tulliallan, inventory, 1810, Comm. Dunblane. [NRS.CC6.W111]

SCOTT, ANDREW, master of the Dorset of Grangemouth trading between Leith and Halifax, Nova Scotia, in 1816. [NRS.E504.22.73]

SCOTT, ANDREW, of the Balfron Emigration Society, Stirlingshire, from Greenock aboard the David of London bound for Quebec, Canada, on 19 May 1821, was granted land in Lanark, Upper Canada on 3 December 1821. [PAO]

SCOTT, HENRY, born 1849, son of William Scott, [1804-1873]. And his wife Bethia Brown, [1806-1878], died in Portland, Victoria, Australia, on 14 April 1883. [Slammannan gravestone, Falkirk, Stirlingshire]

SCOTT, WALTER, MD, born 1840, son of William Scott, [1804-1873], and his wife Bethia Brown, [1806-1878], died in Hamilton, Victoria, Australia, on 19 August 1874. [Slamannan gravestone, Falkirk, Stirlingshire]

SCOTT, WILLIAM, was admitted as a burgess and guilds-brother of Stirling in 1807. [SBR]

SEATON, DAN, from Stirling, a volunteer under Garibaldi in Italy in 1860. [SHR.57.177]

SEATON, JOHN, was admitted as a burgess and guilds-brother of Stirling in 1832. [SBR]

SEATON, THOMAS, a mechanic, was admitted as a burgess of Stirling in 1813. [SBR]

SEGGIE, SAMUEL, in Tullibody, Clackmannanshire, applied to settle in Canada on 27 February 1815. [NRS.RH9]

SHARP, COLIN, a tailor, was admitted as a burgess of Stirling in 1806. [SBR]

SHARP, JOHN, in Craigie, Clackmannan, a victim of rioting etc, there in 1842. [NRS.AD14.42.339]

SHAW, ROBERT, master of the Nancy of Grangemouth, inventory, 1805, Comm. Stirling. [NRS]

SHAW, ROBERT, was admitted as a burgess of Stirling in 1830. [SBR]

SHAW, Reverend WILLIAM, was admitted as a burgess and guilds brother of Stirling in 1804. [SBR]

SHEARER, ROBERT, was admitted as a burgess and guilds-brother of Stirling in 1818. [SBR]

SHEARER, WILLIAM, born 1818, a tailor in Balfron, died in Drymen on 12 October 1900, husband of Ann Johnston, born 1814, died on 30 September 1892. [Balfron gravestone, Stirlingshire]

SHIRRA, JOHN, was admitted as a burgess and guilds-brother of Stirling in 1804. [SBR]

SHIRRA, NICOL, in Rodgerville, Huron County, Canada West, brother and her of Janet Shirra or Harvey in Shirgarton, Kippen, Stirlingshire, in 1870. [NRS.S/H]

SIM, THOMAS, a skipper in Tulliallan, Stirlingshire, testament, 1805, Comm. Dunblane. [NRS]

SIMPSON, ADA, and Elizabeth Simpson, in Pittston, America, nieces and heirs of Alexander Simpson, a spirit merchant in Falkirk, Stirlingshire, who died on 3 July 1874. [NRS.S/H]

SIMPSON, JAMES, born in Grangemouth, Stirlingshire, master of the schooner Samuel Gould of St John, died of yellow fever off New Orleans, Louisiana, on 6 August 1837. [New Brunswick Courier, 16.3.1837]

SIMPSON, MARGARET, wife of Christopher Wallace in Wilkes-Barre, Pennsylvania, niece and joint heir of Alexander Simpson, a spirit merchant in Falkirk, Stirlingshire, who died on 3 July 1874. [NRS.S/H]

SIMPSON, PETER, a skipper in Skinflat, Falkirk, Stirlingshire, an inventory, 1814, Comm. Stirling. [NRS]

SIMPSON, PETER, an acid manufacturer in Camelon, Stirlingshire, died 16 February 1856, uncle of Alexander Simpson in USA his heir. [NRS.S/H]

SIMPSON, WILLIAM, from Stirling, a divinity student in 1825, a minister in Canada. [OSC]

SIMPSON, WILLIAM, [1843-1889], and his wife Janet Honeyman, [1843-1912], parents of William Simpson, born 1871, died in Victoria, British Columbia, on 24 October 1891. [Greenside gravestone, Alloa]

SIMPSON, WILLIAM, a nurseryman in Falkirk, Stirlingshire, died 19 October 1850. [NRS.S/H]

SIMPSON, Captain, master of the Lady Bruce of Grangemouth bound for Australia in July 1853. [LCL.4225]

SKENDLING, THOMAS, died 13 May 1859, husband of Margaret Lundie, born in 1801, died on 27 October 1880. [Alva gravestone, Clackmannanshire]

SMART, JAMES, a cordiner, was admitted as a burgess of Stirling in 1804. [SBR]

SMART, JAMES, of the Relief Congregation in St Ninian's, Stirling, a petition in 1845. [NRS.GD112.B.3.4]

SMART, WILLIAM, a farmer and cattle-dealer in Alva, Clackmannanshire, sequestration in 1850. [NRS.CS280.36.121]

SMITH, ARCHIBALD, a slater at Deanston Mill, Doune, Stirlingshire, Master of the Lodge St James number 171 in 1810. [DHN.iii]

SMITH, HARRIET DUDLEY, born 8 February 1844 in Jackson, Missouri, wife of George R. Ure, died in Bonnybridge on 3 January 1889. [Larbert gravestone, Stirlingshire]

SMITH, HUGH, a merchant in Stirling, testament, 1793, Comm. Stirling. [NRS]

SMITH, JAMES, born 1790, a former apprentice under Sir Richard Arkwright, manager of the Deanston Mill, Doune, Stirlingshire, also an agricultural innovator, and Master of the Lodge St James number 171 from 1818-1819, died in 1850. [DHN.100/iii]

SMITH, JAMES, a minister in Nashville, Kentucky, heir of his uncle James Smith, son of Peter Smith a merchant in Doune, Stirlingshire, dead by 1835. [NRS.S/H]

SMITH, JOHN, of Pinfoldbridge, born 1747, late in the Service of the East India Company, died on 15 September 1828. [Larbert gravestone, Stirlingshire]

SMITH, JOHN, was admitted as a burgess and guilds-brother of Stirling in 1800. [SBR]

SMITH, JOHN, born in 1800, a patternmaker in Carron, died on 18 January 1836, husband of Margaret Watt, born 1802, died on 19 January 1842. [Larbert gravestone, Stirlingshire]

SMITH, JOHN, a collier in Clackmannan, and his wife Catherine, were accused of part of a mobbing, rioting, assaulting officers of the law, and rescuing person from lawful custody in Clackmannan in 1842. [NRS.AD14.42.339]

SMITON, GEORGE, a mechanic, was admitted as a burgess of Stirling in 1807. [SBR]

SNEDDON, DAVID, born 1812, a shipowner, died on 12 February 1878, husband of Allison Harrower, born 1813, died 15 December 1871. [Alloa gravestone, Clackmannanshire]

SNEDDON, JANET, in Lauriston, Falkirk, Stirlingshire, was dead by 1852. [NRS.S/H]

SOMERVILLE, BANKS, was admitted as a burgess and guilds-brother of Stirling in 1820. [SBR]

SOMERVILLE, ELIZA, daughter of John Somerville, died on 11 July 1863, and was buried in Springdale Cemetery, Peoria, Illinois. [Airth, gravestone, Stirlingshire]

SOMERVILLE, JAMES, born 1747, minister of the Scots Kirk in Rotterdam, Zeeland, from 1775 until 1779, later a minister in Stirling from 1789 until his death in 1817. [F.4.321-325]

SORLEY, JAMES, was admitted as a burgess and guilds-brother of Stirling in 1821. [SBR]

SPIERS, JOHN, in Waterloo, Canada, grandson and heir of James Willison a baker in Denny, Stirlingshire, who died in October 1815. [NRS.S/H]

SPOTTISWOOD, THOMAS, of Dunipace, died in 1837. [Falkirk gravestone, Stirlingshire]

STAINTON, JOSEPH, of Biggarshiels, born 1756, manager of the Carron Ironworks from 1786 until his death in 1825. [Larbert gravestone, Stirlingshire]

STALKER, JOHN, was admitted as a burgess and guilds-brother of Stirling in 1823. [SBR]

STARK, Reverend ANDREW, LL.D., from New York, died in Dennyloanhead Manse, Stirlingshire, on 18 September 1849. [SG.18.1858][AJ.5308]

STARK, ARCHIBALD, messenger at arms, Falkirk, Stirlingshire, 1849. [POD]

STARK, THOMAS, was admitted as a burgess and guilds-brother of Stirling in 1813. [SBR]

STEEDMAN, JAMES, a hammerman, was admitted as a burgess of Stirling in 1802. [SBR]

STEEDMAN, ..., a Lieutenant of the Clackmannan Volunteers, was admitted as a burgess and guilds-brother of Dunfermline, Fife, on 24 February 1804. [DM]

STEEL, ADAM, was admitted as a burgess and guilds-brother of Stirling in 1803. [SBR]

STEEL, JEAN, wife of H. Swinton a merchant in Grangemouth, Stirlingshire, was dead by 1847, mother of George Steel Swinton in the Sandwich Islands, [Hawaii]. [NRS.S/H]

STEEN, ANDREW, a Lieutenant of the Clackmannan Volunteers, was admitted as a burgess of Dunfermline, Fife, on 24 February 1804. [DM]

STEVEN, WILLIAM, from Falkirk, Stirlingshire, died in San Fernando, Trinidad, on 25 September 1840. [W.97]

STEVENSON, ALEXANDER, a weaver, was admitted as a burgess of Stirling in 1801. [SBR]

STEVENSON, Reverend ARCHIBALD, son of William Stevenson, [1797-1872], and his wife Isabella ......, [1802-1882], died in St Rennie, Napiervile County, Quebec, on 8 October 1907. [Holy Rude gravestone, Stirling]

STEVENSON, MARY, born 8 October 1809, daughter of Hugh Stevenson and his wife Janet Nelson, died in America in 1892. [St Ninian's gravestone, Stirling]

STEVENSON, PATRICK, a merchant in Stirling, testament, 1798, Comm. Stirling. [NRS]

STEVENSON, SAMUEL, President of the Alloa Emigration Society, with his wife and daughter, from Greenock aboard the David of London bound for Quebec, Canada, on 19 May 1821, was granted land in Lanark, Upper Canada on 10 September 1821. [PAO]

STEWART, AGNES, born 1842 in Balfron, Stirlingshire, died at her home in Reed Street, Oamaru, New Zealand, on 8 February 1885. [S.13020]

STEWART, ANDREW, a shoemaker in Stirling, with his wife and two children, applied to settle in Canada on 19 March 1827. [TNA.CO384.5.1031]

STEWART, CHARLES, agent of the Western Bank in Campsie, Stirlingshire, in 1849. [POD]

STEWART, DANIEL, born 1803, 'sometime of Caluka, Hamiton, Ontario, died on 31 October 1883. [Dunblane gravestone, Stirlingshire]

STEWART, DOUGALD, a merchant in Jamaica, relict of Agnes Muirhead in Falkirk, Stirlingshire, testament, 1795, Comm. Stirling. [NRS]

STEWART, H., born in Stirling, a saddler, died in St George, Grenada, on 3 November 1818. [EA.5744.39]

STEWART, JAMES, a mason, son of Alexander Stewart a shoemaker in Buchany, Doune, Stirlingshire, Master of the Lodge St James number 171 from 1828-1829. [DHN.iii]

STEWART, JOHN, eldest son of John Stewart in Stirling, died in St James, Jamaica, on 25 May 1799. [GC.1264][EA]

STEWART, Captain JOHN, from Alloa, Clackmannanshire, late master of the brig Retreat, died in St John, New Brunswick, on 15 June 1842. [New Brunswick Courier, 18.6.1842]

STEWART, JOHN, of Cornton, born 1752, died on 18 October 1820, husband of Jean Davidson, born 1758, died on 25 November 1789. [Logie Old gravestone, Stirlingshire]

STEWART, PETER, born 1793 in Stirlingshire, a steamboat engineer, died in St John, New Brunswick, on 23 January 1825. [New Brunswick Courier, 29.11.1825]

STEWART, ROBERT, a baker in Callander, Stirlingshire, was accused of 'hamesucken' in 1831. [NRS.AD14.31.4]

STEWART, THOMAS, son of Alexander Stewart a shipmaster in Kincardine, was apprenticed to Allan, Stewart, and Company, merchants in Edinburgh, for five years, in May 1797. [ERA]

STIRLING, GEORGE G., a deed re Burnbank and the Port of Menteith, 20 April 1841. [NRS.RD29.3.23]

STIRLING, JAMES, born 1752, from Stirling, emigrated to America in 1774, settled in Baltimore, Maryland, died on 25 June 1820. [BAF]

STIRLING, or McGREGOR, JANE, in Guelph, Canada, sister and heir of Thomas Stirling, son of Reverend Dr Alexander Stirling in Tillicoutry, Stirlingshire, 1847. [NRS.S/H]

STIRLING, JOHN, second son of William Stirling of Keir, Stirlingshire, died in Jamaica on 24 March 1793. [SM.88.307]

STIRLING, JOHN, born 20 October 1786, son of Andrew Stirling of Drumpellier, was educated at Glasgow University in 1799, married Elizabeth Willing in Philadelphia, Pennsylvania, on 4 February 1816. [MAGU]

STIRLING, MARY ANN, wife of Sir Samuel Stirling of Glorat, died in Friedrichshaffen, Germany, on 8 October 1856. [W.XVII.1811]

STIRLING, ROBERT, a hammerman, was admitted as a burgess of Stirling in 18509. [SBR]

STIRLING, THOMAS, son of Reverend Dr Alexander Stewart in Tillicoultry, Clackmannanshire, was dead by 1847, brother of Jane Stirling or McGregor in Guelph, Canada. [NRS.S/H]

STIRLING, WILLIAM, a hammerman, was admitted as a burgess of Stirling in 1813. [SBR]

STIRLING, WILLIAM, second son of John Stirling of Kippendavie, Stirlingshire, married Elizabeth Barrett, only child of Henry Barrett, of Dollar, Clackmannanshire, in Jamaica on 10 November 1811. [SM.74.155]

STIRTON, GRACE, born 1787, widow of Peter Slater, died in Canada West on 29 December 1878. [Gartmore gravestone, Stirlingshire]

STIVEN, or BLACK, HELEN, in Falkirk, Stirlingshire, was dead by 1845, brother of John Stiven a millwright in Trinidad. [NRS.S/H]

STODDART, PETER, was admitted as a burgess and guilds-brother of Stirling in 1824. [SBR]

STRACHAN, WILLIAM R., son of J. M. Strachan MD in Dollar, Clackmannanshire, died in St Elisabeth's, Jamaica, on 16 August 1860. [S.1638]

STRANG, JAMES, son of David Strang a craftsman in Kippen Stirlingshire, was educated at Glasgow University in 1816, a minister in America. [MAGU]

STRANG, PETER, a tailor, was admitted as a burgess of Stirling in 1808. [SBR]

SUTHERLAND, PATRICK, was admitted as a burgess and guilds-brother of Stirling in 1803. [SBR]

SWAN, ROBERT, was admitted as a burgess and guilds-brother of Stirling in 1804. [SBR]

SWINTON, GEORGE STEEL, in the Sandwich Islands, [Hawaii], son and heir of Jean Steel, wife of H. Swinton a merchant in Grangemouth, Stirlingshire,1847. [NRS.S/H]

SYMMERS, JAMES, in Hamilton, Ontario, nephew and heir of James Symmers, a teacher in Dollar, Clackmannanshire, who died on 31 October 1880. [NRS.S/H]

TAIT, BENJAMIN, died in Connoshaken, USA, 19 November 1840. [SO]

TAIT, THOMAS, was admitted as a burgess and guilds-brother of Stirling in 1827. [SBR]

TAYLOR, ALEXANDER, a manufacturer in Alva, Clackmannanshire, sequestration in 1843, [NRS.CS280.29.146]

TAYLOR, HENRY, in Bannockburn, Stirlingshire, a victim of cattle stealing in 1837. [NRS.AD14.37.528]

TAYLOR, HENRY JOHN, in High Street, Falkirk, Stirlingshire, a victim of theft and reset in 1852. [NRS.AD14.14.52.373]

TAYLOR, JAMES, in Denny, died 18 March 1865, cousin of Andrew Drysdale in Stratford, Ontario. [NRS.S/H]

TAYLOR, JOHN, born 1749, a mason, died 1 March 1813, husband of Mary Moir, born 1757, died 3 April 1827, son Robert Taylor, born 1786, a mason, died 15 March 1863, his wife Catherine Morrison, born 1792, died 26 December 1881, their son John Taylor, born 1822, died 27 February 1829. [Kippen gravestone]

TAYLOR, JOHN, of Ballochneck, Stirlingshire, eldest son of Reverend Dr William Taylor, St Enoch's, Glasgow, died in Bardowie, St Andrew's, Jamaica, on 17 August 1829. [S.1029]; inventory, 1831. [NRS.SC70.1.45]

TAYLOR, JOHN, a labourer in Tillicoultry, Clackmannanshire, dead by 1865, father of Peter Arnot Taylor a cooper in Sparta, North America. [NRS.S/H]

TAYLOR, MATHEW, in High Street, Falkirk, Stirlingshire, a victim of theft and reset in 1852. [NRS.AD14.14.52.373]

TAYLOR, PETER ARNOT, a cooper in Sparta, North America, son and heir of John Taylor a labourer in Tillicoultry, Clackmannanshire, also, to his mother Christian Arnot there, 1865. [NRS.S/H]

TAYLOR, ROBERT, born 1836, a mason, died 25 December 1906. [Kippen gravestone]

TAYLOR, WILLIAM, a skipper from Bowhall in Grangemouth, inventory, 1814, Comm. Stirling. [NRS]

TAYLOR, WILLIAM, born 1775 in Falkirk, Stirlingshire, son of John Taylor a farmer, was educated at Glasgow University, emigrated to Canada, a minister in Osbruck and Williamsburg, Ontario, in 1819, later in Waddington, New York, died 1837. [F][UPC][MAGU]

TAYLOR, WILLIAM, a merchant in Stirling, died there, 30 March 1844] [SO]

TELFORD, ARCHIBALD, a baker, son of James Telford, was admitted as a burgess and guilds-brother of Stirling in 1831. [SBR]

TELFORD, DAVID, was admitted as a burgess and guilds-brother of Stirling in 1804. [SBR]

TELFORD, JAMES, a maltman, was admitted as a burgess and guilds-brother of Stirling in 1812. [SBR]

TEMPLE, ….., Adjutant of the Clackmannan Volunteers, was admitted as a burgess and guilds-brother of Dunfermline, Fife, on 24 February 1804. [DM]

THOMAS, WILLIAM, born in 1798, of the Royal Oak Hotel, died on 17 June 1883. [Clackmannan gravestone]

THOMSON, A., a farmer, died at Myreton, Clackmannan, 20 June 1839. [SO]

THOMSON, ALEXANDER, born 1813, an auctioneer, died 6 May 1879, husband of Margaret Woodburn, born 1816, died on 16 June 1896. [Alloa gravestone, Clackmannanshire]

THOMSON, ANDREW, a Lieutenant of the Clackmannan Volunteers, was admitted as a burgess and guilds-brother of Dunfermline, Fife, on 24 February 1804. [DM]

THOMSON, GEORGE, was accused of assault and robbery in Cow Wynd, Falkirk, Stirlingshire, in 1824. [NRS.AD14.24.234]

THOMSON, Reverend JAMES, born 1724, son of George Thomson a merchant in Falkirk, Stirlingshire, was educated at Glasgow University in 1744, a minister in Dundee from 1761 until 1785, emigrated in 1785, 'laboured sometime in the Lord's work in America', returned to Scotland in 1790, died in Dundee on 17 November 1791. [MAGU] [F.5.328] [Dundee Howff gravestone]

THOMSON, JAMES, of the Alloa Emigration Society, from Greenock aboard the David of London bound for Quebec, Canada, on 19 May 1821, was granted land in Lanark, Upper Canada on 10 September 1821. [PAO]

THOMSON, JAMES, born 1778, for fifty-two years the minister of the Secession Congregation at Holm of Balfron, died 13 November 1864, husband of Janet Dunlop, born 1782, died in February 1864. [Balfron gravestone, Stirlingshire]

THOMSON, JAMES, in Dollar, Clackmannanshire, a petition in 1845. [NRS.GD112.51.181]

THOMSON, JOHN, born 1755 in Stirlingshire, emigrated to New York before 1776, a Loyalist who settled in New Brunswick, died in St John on 23 July 1825. [City Gazette, 26.7.1825]

THOMSON, JOHN, born 12 April 1767 in Falkirk, Stirlingshire, was educated at Edinburgh University, later a schoolmaster in Nova Scotia, then a minister in Bermuda by 1801. [FPA.315] EMA59]

THOMSON, JOHN, born 1777, died 1854, and his wife Agnes Henderson, born 1775, died 1839, parents of James Thomson who died in Melbourne, Victoria, Australia. [Holy Rude gravestone, Stirling]

THOMSON, JOHN, agent of the Edinburgh and Glasgow Bank in Tillicoultry, Clackmannanshire, in 1849. [POD]

THOMSON, MARGARET, widow of John Morison a merchant in Stirling, 1791. Comm. Stirling. [NRS]

THOMSON, PATRICK, a skipper in Kincardine-on-Forth, testament, 1814, Comm. Dunblane. [NRS]

THOMSON, WATSON, born 1789 in Alloa, Clackmannanshire, died in Port Chalmers, New Zealand, on 19 October 1876. [AJ.6729]

THOMSON, WILLIAM, a butcher, was admitted as a burgess and guilds-brother of Stirling in 1800. [SBR]

THOMSON, WILLIAM, a shipmaster in Melbourne, Victoria, Australia, son and heir of Andrew Thomson, a merchant in Alloa, Clackmannanshire, in 1857. [NRS.S/H]

THOMSON, Captain, master of the Duke of Bronte of Alloa from Aberdeen to Quebec in 1856, also from Troon, Ayrshire, to Quebec in 1856. [AJ.5652/5661/5680]

THORBURN, WILLIAM, was admitted as a burgess and guilds-brother of Stirling in 1804. [SBR]

TODD, ANDREW, a manufacturer in Alva, Clackmannanshire, sequestration in 1845. [NRS.CS280.31.78]

TOWART, JOHN, a merchant in Stirling, testament, 1796. Comm. Stirling. [NRS]

TOWERS, GEORGE, was admitted as a burgess of Stirling in 1856. [SBR]

TOWERS, JOHN, a mariner in Carronshore, inventory, 1801, Comm. Stirling. [NRS]

TOWERS, JOHN, a weaver, was admitted as a burgess of Stirling in 1829. [SBR]

TRAQUAIR, PATRICK JOHN, son of John Traquair, was admitted as a burgess and guilds-brother of Stirling in 1842. [SBR]

TRAQUAIR, THOMAS, a mechanic, was admitted as a burgess and guilds-brother of Stirling in 1808. [SBR]; died in Stirling, 14 October 1841. [SO]

TURCAN, ALEXANDER, a skipper in Kincardine-on-Forth, testament, 1809, Comm. Dunblane. [NRS]

TURCAN, JOHN, master of the Jeanie of Kincardine trading between Alloa and Pillau, Germany, in 1817. [NRS.E504.2.13]

TURCAN, WILLIAM, a skipper in Kincardine-on-Forth, inventory, 1803, Comm. Dunblane. [NRS]

TURCAN, WILLIAM, master of the Catherine of Kincardine trading between Alloa and Pillau, Germany, in 1817. [NRS.E504.2.13]

TURCAN, WILLIAM, born 1826, son of George Turcan and his wife Agnes Mercer, died in Rio de Janeiro, Brazil, on 2 March 1852. [Tulliallan gravestone]

TURNBULL, ALEXANDER, born 1805, 'for 71 years was employed at the Carron Ironworks', died on 22 September 1885, husband of Jean Black, born 1810, died 1 August 1902. [Larbert gravestone, Stirlingshire]

TURNBULL, GEORGE, in Dennyloanhead, Stirlingshire, died 21 July 1866, father of Reverend Robert Turnbull in Hartford, North America. [NRS.S/H]

TURNBULL, JAMES, born 1805, son of William Turnbull of Forthbank, [1767-1851], and his wife Jean Colquhoun, [1781-1852], died in Jamaica on 29 August 1807. [St Ninian's gravestone, Stirlingshire]

TURNBULL, JOHN, and his wife Agnes Irvine, parents of John Turnbull, born 1865, died in Newark, New Jersey, on 14 August 1899. [Stirling gravestone]

TURNBULL, ROBERT, a minister in Hartford, North America, son and heir of George Turnbull in Dennyloanhead, Stirlingshire, who died on 21 July 1866. [NRS.S/H]

TURNBULL, WILLIAM, was admitted as a burgess and guilds-brother of Stirling in 1817. [SBR]

TURNBULL, WILLIAM, born 1821, son of William Turnbull of Forthbank, [1767-1851], and his wife Jean Colquhoun, [1781-1852], parents of William Turnbull, born 1821, died in Newmarket, Upper Canada, on 10 March 1847. [St Ninian's gravestone, Stirling]

TURNBULL, WILLIAM, of Forthbank, Stirling, died in Newmarket, Canada, 29 April 1847. [SO]

TURNER, JOHN, a weaver, was admitted as a burgess of Stirling in 1830. [SBR]

TURNER, WILLIAM, Lieutenant of the 93rd Highlanders, died in Varna, Italy, 7 September 1854. [SO]

URE, CHARLES, in High Street, Falkirk, Stirlingshire, a victim of theft and reset in 1852. [NRS.AD14.52,373]

URE, JAMES, Customs Collector at the Port of Alloa, Clackmannanshire, in 1816. [NRS.E504.2.13]

URE, JOHN, [1792-1853], and his wife Margaret Archibald, [1799-1870], parents of John Ure who died in Lawrence, Massachusetts, on 14 April 1898. [Tillicoutry gravestone, Clackmannanshire]

URE, ROBERT, a maltman, was admitted as a burgess of Stirling in 1834. [SBR]

URQUHART, JOHN, messenger at arms in Alloa, Clackmannanshire, in 1849. [POD]

VANCE, CHRISTOPHER, son of John Vance, [1800-1867], and his wife Janet Aitken, [1813-1890], died in South Australia, on 21 September 1882. [Holy Rude gravestone, Stirling, gravestone]

VANCE, HELEN, daughter of John Vance, [1800-1867], and his wife Janet Aitken, [1813-1890], wife of W. Tod Flint, died in Adelaide, South Australia. [Holy Rude gravestone, Stirling]

VANCE, HELEN, daughter of John Vance, [1800-1867], and his wife Janet Aitken, [1813-1890], wife of John Bryce, died in Astoria, Oregon, on 8 April 1878. [Holy Rude gravestone, Stirling]

VINT, BENJAMIN, in Campsie, Stirlingshire, a former soldier of the 42nd Regiment of Foot [the Black Watch], applied to settle in Canada on 28 May 1827. [TNA.CO384.5.1059]

VIRTUE, ALEXANDER, postmaster at Bridge of Allan, Stiringshire, died there, 29 March 1849. [SO]

VIRTUE, JOHN MCLEAN, in Bridge of Allan, Stirlingshire, died there, 3 April 1845. [SO]; born 1806, in Bridge of Allan, died on 15 March 1849, husband of Betsy Jennison McQueen, born 1807, died 29 May 1874. [Logie Old gravestone, Stirlingshire]

WADDLE, GEORGE, an Excise officer, died in Grangemouth, Stirlingshire, 28 May 1846. [SO]

WADDEL, JAMES, was admitted as a burgess and guilds-brother of Stirling in 1804. [SBR]

WALKER, GEORGE, a minister from Falkirk, Stirlingshire, died in New York, 16 March 1843. [SO]

WALKER GEORGE AUSTIN MIDDLETON, son of George Austin Walker, MD, [1816-1891], and his wife Margaret Logan, [1869-1893], died in Bolivia in 1874. [Dollar gravestone, Clackmannanshire]

WALKER, HUGH, of Carron Hall, died in Jamaica on 17 August 1820. [AJ.3801]

WALKER, JOHN, factor to the Earl of Moray, also Baron Bailie of Doune, Master of the Lodge St James number 171 from 1806 until 1807. [DHN.iii]

WALKER, JOHN DICKSON, born 1834, son of James Walker, [1787-1871], and his wife Jane Smith, [died 1831], died in Quebec on 3 August 1854. [Dollar gravestone, Clackmannanshire]

WALKER, PETER, a merchant from Stirling but in New York, nephew and heir of Robert Walker a merchant in Aberdeen, in 1835. [NRS.S/H]

WALKER, ROBERT, born 1831, a teacher in the Free Church school in Kenmore, died 15 March 1859, brother of Ann Walker, born 1845, died 1 April 1859. [Falkirk gravestone, Stirlingshire]

WALKER, THOMAS, in Claybank, Denny, Stirlingshire, a victim of cattle stealing in 1837. [NRS.AD14.37.528]

WALLS, ARCHIBALD, a smith in St Ninian's, Stirling, died there, 19 January 1854. [SO]

WANDS, JOHN, a weaver, was admitted as a burgess of Stirling in 1819. [SBR]

WARDLAW, HENRY, an Excise officer, died on 21 July 1820, husband of Jean Guild, who died on 9 January 1847. [Dollar gravestone, Clackmannanshire]

WARDROP, ELIZABETH, spouse of Thomas Henderson of Blairs residing in Stirling, testament, 1793, Comm. Stirling. [NRS]

WATERS, THOMAS, born 1736, first minister of the West Alloa United Presbyterian congregation, died 1 May 1809. [Alloa, gravestone, Clackmannanshire]

WATERS, Miss, died in Chicago, Illinois, 21 October 1852. [SO]

WATSON, MARGARET, daughter of John Watson a merchant in Alloa, married James Ferguson, a writer in Edinburgh on 14 April 1783. A Declarator of Marriage in 1785. [NRS.CC8.6.734]

WATSON, ROBERT, a teacher in Dunipace, Stirlingshire, died there, 25 May 1854. [SO]

WATT, ALEXANDER, born 1767 in Carron, Stirlingshire, a mariner who was naturalised in Charleston, South Carolina, on 2 November 1803. [NARA.M1183.1]

WATT, ARCHIBALD, a baker, was admitted as a burgess of Stirling in 1808. [SBR]

WATT, GEORGE, of the Alloa Emigration Society, with his wife and family, from Greenock aboard the David of London bound for Quebec, Canada, on 19 May 1821, was granted land in Lanark, Upper Canada in 1821. [PAO]

WATT, JAMES, master of the Sisters of Kincardine trading between Alloa and Archangel, Russia, in 1817. [NRS.E504.2.13]

WAUGH, ANNE, eldest daughter of Patrick Waugh of Arbuthnott Cottage, Stirlingshire, and of Dromilly Estate, Trelawney, Jamaica, married James Murray in Georgia Estate, Trelawney, Jamaica, on 24 September 1840. [AJ.4848]

WAUCH, JAMES, a Lieutenant of the Loyal Stirling Volunteers, was admitted as a burgess and guilds-brother of Dunfermline, Fife, on 17 July 1804. [DM]

WEDDERSPOON, JOSEPH, a mechanic, was admitted as a burgess of Stirling in 1818. [SBR]

WEIR, DANIEL, son of Thomas Weir in Kerse, a merchant who died in Demerara in January 1793. [SM.55.163]

WEIR, GEORGE, of Kames, died In St Denis, Canada, 18 January 1838. [SO]

WEIR, JAMES, born 1782, a farmer from Barrachan, New Kilpatrick, Stirlingshire, emigrated via Greenock aboard the Mary, Captain Moore, bound for Canada in 1817. [TNA.CO384.1]

WEIR, JOHN BLACKWOOD, in Torwoodhall, Canada, son and heir of Helen Blackwood, wife of John Weir in Grahamston, Falkirk, Stirlingshire; also, heir to his brother Jmes Weir, a merchant in Dundas, Wentworth, Canada, in 1853. [NRS.S/H]

WEIR, ROBERT, born 1809, son of Robert Weir, a merchant in Glasgow, and his wife Janet Barry, died in Montreal, Quebec, on 10 May 1843. [Denny gravestone, Stirlingshire]

WEIR, THOMAS, a surgeon, died 24 February 1851, his wife Annabella Rennie, died 9 April 1852. [Kippen gravestone, Stirlingshire]

WEST, GEORGE, was admitted as a burgess and guilds-brother of Stirling in 1818. [SBR]

WHITE, ARCHIBALD, born 1757, parochial teacher in Alloa for 20 years, died in December 1806, husband of Helen Johnstone, born 1754, died 1814, parents of John White, a surgeon in the Service of the East India Company, who died in London on 12 November 1873. [Alloa gravestone, Clackmannanshire]

WHITE, ELIZABETH, in Goshen, Dereham, Canada West, heir of Mary Lang, wife of William Rennie in Kilsyth, Stirlingshire, who died on 27 May 1832. [NRS.S/H]

WHITE, JAMES, from New Sauchie, Stirlingshire, emigrated via Dundee aboard the clipper ship Duntrune, master John Rollo, on 1 September 1883, landed at Moreton Bay, Brisbane, Queensland, Australia, in December 1883. [DPL.ms.405]

WHITE, JAMES, and his wife Marion Duncan, were parents of William White, born 1857, died in Melbourne, Victoria, Australia, on 6 July 1888. [St Ninian's gravestone, Stirling]

WHITE, JANET, in Goshen, Dereham, Canada West, heir of her grand-aunt Mary Lang, wife of William Rennie in Kilsyth, Stirlingshire, who died on 27 May 1832. [NRS.S/H]

WHITE, JOHN, master of the Kaims of Alloa trading between Alloa and Belfast, Ireland, in 1816. [NRS.E504.2.13]

WHITE, MELISSA, in Goshen, Dereham, Canada West, heir of Mary Lang, wife of William Rennie in Kilsyth, Stirlingshire, who died on 27 May 1832. [NRS.S/H]

WHITE, ROBERT, son of James White a wright in Falkirk, Stirlingshire, was apprenticed to James Wright, a pewterer in Edinburgh, for six years, on 23 May 1793. [ERA]

WHITE, ROBERT, in Goshen, Dereham, Canada West, heir of Mary Lang, wife of William Rennie in Kilsyth, Stirlingshire, who died on 27 May 1832. [NRS.S/H]

WHITEHEAD, ALEXANDER, born in St Ninian's, Stirling, in 1756, emigrated to America, Master of Norfolk Academy in Virginia, later, Rector of the parish of Elizabeth River, Va., in 1789, studied medicine at Glasgow University in 1798, a doctor in Norfolk, Va., died in 1826. [OD][SA]

WHITEHEAD, ARCHIBALD, a multurer at the Bridge of Stirling, testament, 1793, Comm. Stirling. [NRS]

WHITEHEAD, ARCHIBALD, a baker, was admitted as a burgess of Stirling in 1816. [SBR]

WHITEHEAD, JAMES, born in St Ninian's, Stirling, was educated at Glasgow University, emigrated to America, Rector of the parish of Elizabeth River, Va., and master of Norfolk Academy in 1792 [OD]

WILKIE, HELEN, in St Kitts, heir to her grand-mother Helen Napier, wife of J. Forrester in Stirling Castle, in 1816. [NRS.S/H]

WILLIAMS, or BURNS, ELIZABETH, from Falkirk, found guilty of reset in Stirling on 9 September 1811, sentenced to transportation to the colonies for fourteen years. [SM.83.10/790]

WILLIAMSON, ALEXANDER, born 5 December 1829 in Falkirk, was educated at Glasgow University in 1853, a missionary of the United Presbyterian Church in Chefoo, China, from 1870 until his death there on 2 September 1890. [RGG.646]

WILLIAMSON, JAMES, a weaver in Alva, Stirlingshire, was accused of poaching in 1844. [NRS.AD14.44.390]

WILLIAMSON, MARTHA, relict of John Muschet a minister in Stirling, testament, 1796, Comm. Stirling. [NRS]

WILLIAMSON, ROBERT, a clock and watchmaker in Falkirk from 1818 until 1841. [OSC.109]

WILLIS, GEORGE, was admitted as a burgess and guilds-brother of Stirling in 1804. [SBR]

WILLIS, ROBERT, was admitted as a burgess and guilds-brother of Stirling in 1805. [SBR]

WILLISON, JAMES, a baker in Denny, Stirlingshire, died in October 1815. [NRS.S/H.1851]

WILLISON, JOHN, a maltman, was admitted as a burgess and guilds-brother of Stirling in 1808. [SBR]

WILSON, ALEXANDER, born 1754, a shipowner on Carronshore, died in 1815, [Larbert gravestone, Stirlingshire];a shipmaster on Carronshore, inventory, 1819, Comm. Stirling. [NRS]

WILSON, ALEXANDER, born 1832, died in the wreck of the steamship Royal Charter off the coast of Wales, on passage home from Australia on 26 October 1859. [Larbert gravestone, Stirlingshire]

WILSON, DAVID, from Stirlingshire, settled in South Carolina in 1825, was naturalised in Newberry, South Carolina, on 25 April 1829. [S.C. Citizenship book, 119]

WILSON, JAMES, eldest son of John Wilson in Stirling, died in Charleston, South Carolina, on 7 September 1804. [SM.67.973]

WILSON, JOHN, in Bannockburn, was admitted as a burgess and guilds-brother of Stirling in 1808. [SBR]

WILSON, ROBERT, a merchant and innkeeper in Stirling, testaments, 1791, 1796. Comm. Stirling. [NRS]

WILSON, JAMES, eldest son of John Wilson in Stirling, died in Charleston, South Carolina, on 7 September 1804. [SM.66.973] [AJ.2971]

WILSON, THOMAS, son of Reverence Dr James Wilson in Falkirk, Stirlingshire, died in Grenada in June 1805. [AJ.3012][SM.67.805]

WINGATE, DANIEL, was admitted as a burgess and guilds-brother of Stirling in 1802. [SBR]

WINGATE, JAMES, a vintner in Stirling, a testament 1795. [Comm. Stirling. [NRS]

WINGATE, JAMES, born 1830, son of Andrew Wingate in Bankhead, Blair Drummond, Stirlingshire, an ironmonger in Auckland, New Zealand, died in Otahuhu, N.Z., on 10 December 1897. [S.17037]

WINGATE, JOHN, son of Reverend John Wingate in Denny, was apprenticed to Patrick Murray, a goldsmith burgess of Edinburgh on 17 September 1793. [ERA]

WINGATE, JOHN, an ironmonger in Alva, married Isabella Drysdale, there, 8 February 1838. [SO]

WINGATE, THOMAS, was admitted as a burgess and guilds-brother of Stirling in 1801. [SBR]

WINNING, THOMAS, portioner of Balmore, Stirlingshire, died 6 October 1852, father of Ellen Winning, wife of William Jackson a farmer in Handcock, Illinois. [NRS.S/H]

WOOD, JOHN, a merchant and sailor in Alloa, testament, 30 December 1782, Comm. Stirling. [NRS]

WOOD, JOHN, from Slamannan, Stirlingshire, married Janet Hepburn, younger daughter of John Hepburn, in Whitby, Canada West, on 18 May 1857. [EEC.21078]

WOODROW, ANDREW, born 1789, in Lower Shields, died 19 March 1866, husband of Janet Allan, born 1795, died 16 January 1870, parents of John Woodrow who died in Jamaica in March 1868, and Andrew Woodrow, born 1830, who died in Jamaica in May 1869. [Campsie gravestone, Stirlingshire]

WORDIE, WILLIAM, was admitted as a burgess of Stirling in 1839. [SBR]

WRIGHT, DUNCAN, a shipmaster in Kincardine-on-Forth, inventory, 1801, Comm. Dunblane. [NRS]

WRIGHT, or MCBEATH, HELEN, a gardener in Stirling, dead by 1834, mother of James McBeath in New York. [NRS.S/H]

WRIGHT, JAMES, of Loss, Stirling, testament, 1797, Comm. Stirling. [NRS]

WRIGHT, JOHN, and Christian Douglas, 1809. [Falkirk gravestone, Stirlingshire]

WRIGHT, JOHN, born 1780, died 29 April 1867, husband of Ann Forbes, born 1781, died 10 August 1855. [Alloa gravestone, Clackmannanshire]

WRIGHT, MALCOLM, a weaver, was admitted as a burgess of Stirling in 1804. [SBR]

WRIGHT, ROBERT, born 1791, died 1873, and his wife Isabella Parlan, born 1796, died 1869, parents of Robert Wright who died in Australia. [Gargunnock gravestone, Stirlingshire]

WYLD, ALEXANDER, was admitted as a burgess and guilds-brother of Stirling in 1813. [SBR]

WYLD, THOMAS, died in Australia, 5 November 1840. [SO]

WYSE, ARCHIBALD, a jeweller and hardware merchant in Falkirk, died there, 10 October 1839. [SO]Y

WYSE, JAMES, a clock and watchmaker in Falkirk around 1830. [OSC.108]

WYLLIE, ROBERT, master of the Marjory of Kincardine trading between Inverkeithing and Alloa in 1817. [NRS.E504.2.13]

YATES, ELIZABETH, died in Stirling, 4 December 1851. [SO]

YELLOWLEES, DAVID, was admitted as a burgess of Stirling in 1833. [SBR]

YOUNG, ANDREW, a collier in Alloa, Clackmannanshire, was admitted as a burgess and guilds-brother of Dunfermline on 17 April 1793. [DM]

YOUNG, CHARLES, born 1838, eldest son of John Young a writer in Stirling, died in Maryborough, Queensland, Australia, on 21 November 1884. [S.12971]

YOUNG, JAMES, portioner of Torwoodhead, Stirlingshire, died in April 1818, father of James Young in Port Huron, USA. [NRS.S/H]

YOUNG, JOHN, born in September 1773, son of William Young a merchant in Falkirk, Stirlingshire, was educated at Glasgow University in 1790, settled in Nova Scotia as a merchant in 1814, father of William, George, and Charles, an Assemblyman, died in Halifax, N.S., in October 1837. [MAGU] [BNA]

YOUNG, JOHN, of Culimore, Stirling, Judge of the 10th Judicial District of Pennsylvania, died in Greensburg, Pa., on 6 October 1840. [FH.995][AJ.4865][SO.8.4.1841]

YOUNGE, JOHN, minister of the Episcopal chapel in Alloa, died at Shawpark, Alloa, 15 January 1846. [SO]

YOUNG, ROBERT, an innkeeper in Dennyloanhead, Stirlingshire, died there, 7 June 1838. [SO]

YOUNG, ROBERT, a wool-sorter in Tillicoultry, Clackmannanshire, was accused of theft in 1840. [NRS.AD14.40.416]

YOUNG, THOMAS, master of the Fame of Kincardine trading between Pillau, Germany, and Alloa, Clackmannanshire, in 1817. [NRS.E504.2.13]

YOUNG, WILLIAM, a mariner in Falkirk, Stirlingshire, testament, 22 February 1788, Comm. Stirling. [NRS]

YOUNG, WILLIAM, was admitted as a burgess of Stirling in 1825. [SBR]

YOUNG, WILLIAM, a weaver in Alva, Stirlingshire, was accused of poaching in 1844. [NRS.AD14.44.390]

YOUNG, Mrs WILLIAM, born 1742, died in Falkirk, Stirlingshire, on 10 November 1820. [AR.17.3.1821]

YOUNG, Sir WILLIAM, born 29 July 1799 in Falkirk, Stirlingshire, son of John Young a merchant in Glasgow, was educated at Glasgow University in 1813, a barrister and politician in Nova Scotia, died in Halifax, N.S., on 8 May 1887. [MAGU]died in Alloa,

YOUNG, WILLIAM, born 1798, a watchmaker in Stirling, died 1848. [OSC.107]

YOUNG, WILLIAM, son of John Young in Kilsyth, Stirlingshire, emigrated via Greenock bound for Port Phillip, Victoria, Australia, in 1848. [NRS.GD171.1327.2]

YOUNG, Captain, master of the Retreat of Alloa from Alloa, Clackmannanshire, bound for Quebec in 1859. [LCL]

YOUNGER, JOHN, born 1837, son of George Younger, [1790-1853], brewer in Alloa, Clackmannanshire, and his wife Jane Hunter, [1792-....], died in Buenos Ayres, Argentina, in 1865. [SNQ.III.136]

YOUNGER, MARY, died in Alloa, Clackmannanshire, 30 June 1853. [SO]

YUILL, HELEN, a collier in Duke Street, Clackmannan, was accused of part of a mobbing, rioting, assaulting officers of the law, and rescuing person from lawful custody in Clackmannan in 1842. [NRS.AD14.42.339]

YUILL, WILLIAM, of Tipperdarroch and Easter Garden, born 6 April 1804, died at Buchlyvie, Stirlingshire, on 8 May 1884, husband of Margaret Graham, born 27 March 1829, died 26 June 1904. [Kippen gravestone, Stirlingshire]

REFERENCES

CFG Chronicles of the Family of Gairdner

DC Edinburgh Daily Courant, series

DF Family Record of Dingwall and Fordyce

DHN Doune Historical Notes, [Stirling, 1984]

DM Dunfermline Museum

DPCA Dundee, Perth, and Cupar Advertiser, series

DPL Dundee Public Library

GH Glasgow Herald, series

HT History of Tatamagouche, [Halifax, NS, 1917]

LCL Leith Commercial Lists, series

OSC Old Stirling Clockmakers, [Stirling, 1990]s

POD Post Office Directory

SC The Scotsman in Canada, [Toronto, 1911]

SG Scottish Genealogist, series

SJA Stirling Journal and Advertiser

SNQ Scottish Notes and Queries, series

SO Stirling Observer, series

TSR The Scottish Radicals, [Australia, 1981]

www.ingramcontent.com/pod-product-compliance
Lightning Source LLC
Chambersburg PA
CBHW051945160426
43198CB00013B/2301